I0479116

The Ultimate Funnel Marketing Guide:

Attract, Engage, and Convert Customers.

Chapter 1: Introduction to Funnel Marketing

Funnel marketing is a marketing strategy that focuses on guiding potential customers through a series of stages, or "funnel," to convert them into paying customers. It involves creating a systematic process that leads potential customers towards making a purchase, from initial awareness to final conversion.

The concept of funnel marketing is based on the idea that not all potential customers are ready to make a purchase immediately. Instead, they go through a process of becoming aware of a product or service, evaluating it, and then finally deciding to make a purchase. Funnel marketing aims to guide potential customers through this process, using a variety of marketing tactics and techniques.

The funnel typically consists of several stages, including awareness, interest, consideration, and action. At each stage, different marketing strategies are used to move potential customers further down the funnel towards conversion. For example, at the awareness stage, the goal is to make potential customers aware of the product or service. This can be done through various marketing channels such as social media, email marketing, and paid advertising.

As potential customers move further down the funnel, the marketing strategies become more targeted and personalized to their specific needs and interests. For example, at the consideration stage, potential customers may be offered free trials, demos, or consultations to help them evaluate the product or service.

The goal of funnel marketing is to create a seamless and effective process that guides potential customers towards making a purchase. By providing valuable information, personalized experiences, and targeted offers, businesses can increase their conversion rates and improve their bottom line.

In the following chapters, we will dive deeper into the various stages of the funnel and explore specific marketing strategies and tactics that can be used to optimize each stage. Whether you are a small business owner, a marketer, or an entrepreneur, funnel marketing can help you grow your business and achieve your goals.

Chapter 2: Understanding the Buyer's Journey

To create an effective funnel marketing strategy, it's important to understand the buyer's journey. The buyer's journey is the process that potential customers go through when making a purchasing decision. It consists of three main stages: awareness, consideration, and decision.

Awareness Stage: The awareness stage is when a potential customer first becomes aware of a problem or need they have. They may not be aware of a specific solution yet, but they are looking for information and options. At this stage, your goal as a marketer is to raise awareness about your product or service and how it can help solve the potential customer's problem.

Consideration Stage: The consideration stage is when a potential customer is actively researching and considering different options to solve their problem or meet their need. They are evaluating the pros and cons of each choice and trying to decide which one is the best fit for them. At this stage, your goal is to provide valuable information and demonstrate how your product or service is the best option for their needs.

Decision Stage: The decision stage is when a potential customer has made the decision to purchase a product or service. At this stage, your goal is to make the purchasing process as easy and seamless as possible. You want to provide a smooth and enjoyable experience that confirms the customer made the right decision in choosing your product or service.

As a business owner or marketer, understanding your customer's journey is crucial in creating an effective marketing strategy. By acknowledging the different stages of the funnel, you can tailor your marketing tactics and strategies to meet the needs of your customers at each stage.

The awareness stage is the first stage of the funnel, where potential customers become aware of your product or service. This is the time to create brand awareness and build relationships with your target audience. At this stage, social media and content marketing are powerful tools to raise awareness about your brand and showcase your expertise in the industry. By providing valuable and informative content through social media platforms or blog posts, you can establish your brand as a thought leader in the industry and build trust with your audience.

The consideration stage is where potential customers are evaluating your product or service. This is the time to demonstrate the value of your offering and provide solutions to their problems. Offering free trials, demos, or consultations can be a powerful way to help potential customers evaluate your product or service and show them how it can meet their needs. By providing an exceptional experience at this stage, you can build trust with potential customers and increase their likelihood of becoming paying customers.

At the decision stage, potential customers are ready to make a purchase decision. This is the time to focus on providing excellent customer service and incentivizing them to make a purchase. Offering promotions or discounts can be an effective way to encourage customers to make a purchase decision. By providing a seamless and personalized experience throughout the decision-making process, you can build customer loyalty and increase the likelihood of repeat business.

In summary, tailoring your marketing tactics and strategies to each stage of the buyer's journey can increase your conversion rates and create a more effective funnel marketing strategy. By providing valuable information and experiences at each stage, you can establish your brand as a thought leader in the industry, build trust with potential customers, and encourage them to become loyal customers. So, invest your time and resources to understand your customer's journey and create an effective marketing strategy that meets their needs at each stage.

Chapter 3: Identifying Your Target Audience

One of the key components of an effective funnel marketing strategy is identifying your target audience. Your target audience is the group of people who are most likely to be interested in your product or service and who are most likely to make a purchase.

Identifying your target audience involves several steps:

Conduct Market Research

Conducting market research is a crucial step in developing a successful funnel marketing strategy. By gathering insights into your target audience's needs, preferences, and behaviour, you can create tailored messaging and experiences that resonate with them and drive conversions.

There are various methods of conducting market research, such as surveys, focus groups, and customer feedback. Surveys can be conducted online or offline and can gather data on demographics, buying behaviour, and product preferences. Focus groups involve a small group of people discussing their experiences and opinions on a particular topic or product. Customer feedback can be gathered through social media, email, or reviews and can provide valuable insights into your customers' likes, dislikes, and pain points.

When conducting market research, it's essential to analyse and interpret the data gathered to identify patterns, trends, and opportunities. This information can then be used to inform the development of your funnel marketing strategy, including messaging, content, and targeting.

By investing time and resources into market research, you can create a more targeted and effective funnel marketing strategy. This, in turn, can help you drive conversions, build brand loyalty, and grow your business over time. Don't overlook the importance of market research and take the time to understand your audience to create a more effective funnel marketing strategy.

Analyse Your Existing Customer Base

In addition to conducting market research, it's also important to analyse your existing customer base to identify patterns and characteristics that can help you refine your target audience. By looking at the demographics, psychographics, and behaviour of your current customers, you can gain valuable insights that can inform your marketing strategies and help you attract similar customers.

Start by examining your customer database and finding commonalities among your customers, such as age, gender, location, interests, and buying habits. You can use this information to create customer personas, which are fictional representations of your ideal customers. By understanding your ideal customer's needs, pain points, and preferences, you can create more targeted and relevant marketing messages that resonate with them.

Another way to analyse your existing customer base is to conduct customer surveys or interviews to gather feedback about their experience with your product or service. This can help you identify areas for improvement and understand what motivates your customers to purchase from you. You can also use this feedback to identify potential opportunities to expand your offerings or create new products or services that meet the needs of your target audience.

In addition to analysing your existing customer base, you can also leverage data from your website and social media analytics to gain insights into your audience's behaviour and preferences. By tracking metrics such as bounce rates, time on site, and click-through rates, you can gain insights into which content and messaging resonates with your audience and adjust your marketing strategies accordingly.

By taking the time to analyse your existing customer base, you can refine your target audience and create more effective marketing strategies that drive results.

Define Your Ideal Customer Persona

Defining your ideal customer persona is a crucial step in identifying your target audience. Without a clear understanding of who your target audience is, it can be challenging to create effective marketing campaigns that resonate with them.

To define your ideal customer persona, start by collecting as much data as possible about your existing customers. Analyse their demographics, such as age, gender, income, and location, as well as their behaviours, interests, and pain points. You can use tools like surveys, focus groups, and customer feedback to gather this information.

Once you have collected this data, you can start to create a profile of your ideal customer persona. Think about what motivates them, what challenges they face, and how your product or service can help solve their problems. Consider their goals and aspirations and how your product or service can help them achieve those goals.

When creating your ideal customer persona, be as specific as possible. Give them a name, a job title, and a backstory. This will help you to create a more personal connection with your audience and tailor your marketing campaigns to their specific needs.

Keep in mind that your ideal customer persona may evolve over time as your business grows and changes. It's essential to regularly review and update your persona to ensure that it remains relevant and accurate.

Having a clear understanding of your ideal customer persona can help you create more effective marketing campaigns that speak directly to your target audience. By tailoring your messaging and tactics to their specific needs and preferences, you can increase engagement and conversion rates, ultimately driving business growth and success.

Refine Your Target Audience:

Refining your target audience is a crucial step in creating an effective funnel marketing strategy. Once you have conducted market research and gathered information about your potential customers, it's important to analyse and narrow down your target audience to those who are most likely to be interested in your product or service.

One way to refine your target audience is by creating buyer personas, which are detailed descriptions of your ideal customers. These personas include information such as demographics, behaviours, interests, and pain points. By creating personas, you can better understand your target audience's motivations and needs, and tailor your marketing messages to resonate with them.

Another way to refine your target audience is by analysing data from your website and social media analytics. This data can provide insights into the characteristics and behaviours of your website visitors and social media followers, such as their age, gender, location, interests, and the pages they visit the most. You can use this information to refine your buyer personas and adjust your marketing strategies accordingly.

Once you have refined your target audience, it's important to keep them in mind throughout the rest of the funnel marketing process. Consider how your messaging, offers, and call-to-actions will appeal to your target audience, and make sure your marketing efforts are aligned with their needs and preferences.

By refining your target audience, you can create a more effective and efficient funnel marketing strategy that is tailored to the specific needs and interests of your ideal customers. This will help you to better engage with your target audience and ultimately increase your conversion rates.

Once you have identified your target audience, you can tailor your marketing messages and strategies to their specific needs and interests. By speaking directly to your target audience, you can increase engagement and conversions, and ultimately drive more revenue for your business.

Chapter 4: Creating Awareness through Content Marketing

Content marketing is an effective way to create awareness about your product or service and attract potential customers to your website. Content marketing involves creating and sharing valuable, relevant, and consistent content that is designed to attract and retain a specific audience.

Here are some tips for creating effective content marketing:

Identify Your Target Audience

Before creating content for your marketing funnel, it's important to identify your target audience. This involves researching and understanding the demographics, interests, and pain points of the people you want to reach. By understanding your target audience, you can tailor your content to their specific needs and interests, making it more likely that they will engage with your brand.

One way to identify your target audience is to create buyer personas. As mentioned in the earlier chapter to create a buyer persona you can start by gathering data about your existing customers. This can include information such as age, gender, location, occupation, and income level. You can also gather information about their interests and behaviour by analysing their interactions with your brand, such as which pages they visit on your website, what content they engage with, and what products or services they purchase.

Once you have gathered this information, you can use it to create a detailed buyer persona. Give your persona a name and a picture to make it more real and tangible. Then, use the persona to guide your content creation and marketing strategies. For example, if your persona is a working mother in her 30s with a busy schedule, you might create content that offers time-saving tips and advice for managing a work-life balance.

By identifying your target audience and creating buyer personas, you can create content that speaks directly to their needs and interests, making it more likely that they will engage with your brand and move further down the marketing funnel.

Choose Your Content Types

one of the key steps in creating awareness through content marketing is choosing the right content types. While there are many different types of content to choose from, not all will be effective for your specific target audience and business goals.

To begin, consider the type of content that your audience engages with most frequently. Do they prefer blog posts, videos, infographics, or something else? This can be determined through market research and analysis of your audience's behaviour online. Once you have an idea of what type of content they prefer, you can begin to create a content marketing strategy that aligns with those preferences.

Another important factor to consider is the goals of your content. Are you aiming to educate your audience, entertain them, or both? Are you trying to drive traffic to your website or increase brand awareness? Different types of content will be more effective at achieving different goals, so it's important to have a clear understanding of your objectives.

Some popular content types for creating awareness include blog posts, social media posts, videos, infographics, podcasts, and webinars. Each of these types of content has its own unique benefits and can be used to target different stages of the buyer's journey. For example, blog posts and social media posts are great for creating awareness, while webinars and demos are more effective for the consideration stage.

It's also important to keep in mind that the type of content you choose will depend on your resources and budget. While high-quality videos and webinars may be effective, they also require a significant investment of time and money. On the other hand, blog posts and social media posts are relatively easy and inexpensive to create.

Ultimately, the key to choosing the right content types is understanding your audience and goals, and creating content that resonates with both. By taking the time to research and analyse your audience, and by experimenting with different types of content, you can create a content marketing strategy that effectively raises awareness and engages your target audience.

Develop a Content Strategy.

Creating awareness through content marketing requires a well-defined content strategy that is aligned with your business goals and objectives. This strategy should include the topics you will cover, the types of content you will create, and the channels you will use to promote your content.

To develop a successful content strategy, you need to understand your target audience, their needs and interests, and what type of content they engage with the most. You can conduct surveys, polls, or interviews with your existing customers or prospects to gather insights into their preferences and pain points. You can also use analytics tools to analyse your website and social media traffic to determine what type of content drives the most engagement.

Once you have a good understanding of your target audience, you can begin to develop your content strategy. Start by identifying the topics that align with your business goals and resonate with your audience. You can also use keyword research tools to identify the most relevant and popular topics in your industry.

Next, determine the types of content that will work best for each topic. Will it be a blog post, a video, an infographic, a podcast, or something else? Consider the format that best suits the topic and your target audience's preferences.

Finally, consider the channels you will use to promote your content. Social media is an effective platform for sharing your content and reaching a wider audience. You can also use email marketing, guest posting, influencer marketing, and other tactics to increase the visibility of your content.

By developing a content strategy that aligns with your business goals and target audience's interests, you can create compelling content that attracts and engages potential customers. This will help you to build brand awareness, establish thought leadership, and ultimately drive more traffic to your website and generate more leads for your funnel.

Create Quality Content.

Creating quality content is an essential part of your funnel marketing strategy, especially during the awareness stage. Your goal is to provide your target audience with content that is not only engaging but also adds value to their lives.

When creating content, it's important to focus on your audience's pain points and interests. Start by identifying the topics and issues that are most relevant to them. Conducting keyword research and social media listening can help you understand the types of content that your audience is searching for and engaging with.

Once you have identified the topics and interests of your audience, create high-quality content that addresses those pain points and interests. This could be educational, entertaining, or informative content, such as blog posts, videos, podcasts, or social media posts. Your content should provide value to your audience and help them solve their problems or achieve their goals.

It's also essential to ensure that your content is visually appealing and easy to read. Use eye-catching visuals and break up text with headings, bullet points, and images to make it more digestible.

By creating quality content that provides value to your target audience, you can establish yourself as a trusted authority in your industry and increase brand awareness. Additionally, when you create valuable content, your audience is more likely to share it with others, which can lead to increased traffic and engagement on your website and social media channels.

In summary, creating quality content is a critical component of your funnel marketing strategy. By addressing your audience's pain points and interests and providing value through your content, you can build trust with your audience and increase brand awareness.

Promote Your Content.

Creating valuable content is a crucial component of any effective funnel marketing strategy. However, it's not enough to simply create content and hope that your target audience will find it. To ensure your content is reaching the right people, you need to actively promote it.

There are many ways to promote your content, but social media and email marketing are two of the most effective channels. Social media allows you to reach a wider audience and engage with potential customers, while email marketing allows you to reach people who have already expressed interest in your brand.

When promoting your content on social media, it's important to choose the right platforms for your target audience. For example, if you're targeting a younger demographic, you might focus on platforms like TikTok and Instagram. If you're targeting professionals, LinkedIn might be a better choice. Once you've chosen your platforms, you can use paid advertising and organic posting to promote your content and increase visibility.

Email marketing is another powerful way to promote your content. By building an email list of people who have opted-in to receive communications from your brand, you can deliver your content directly to their inbox. This not only increases visibility, but also helps to build trust and rapport with potential customers.

Other channels to consider for content promotion include influencer marketing, guest blogging, and online communities related to your niche. By promoting your content through a variety of channels, you can reach a wider audience and drive more traffic to your website.

In summary, creating valuable content is just the first step in your content marketing strategy. To ensure your content is reaching the right people, you need to actively promote it through social media, email marketing, and other channels. By doing so, you can increase visibility, drive traffic, and ultimately, generate more leads and conversions for your business.

By creating valuable and relevant content, you can establish your brand as a thought leader in your industry and attract potential customers to your website. As these potential customers move through the funnel, you can use targeted content to further engage them and move them towards conversion.

Chapter 5: Generating Leads with Lead Magnets

Lead magnets are a powerful tool for generating leads and building your email list. A lead magnet is a free piece of content or service that you offer in exchange for a potential customer's contact information, such as their email address.

Here are some tips for creating effective lead magnets:

1. Your lead magnet should provide real value to your potential customers. It should solve a problem or answer a question they have, and be something that they can't easily find elsewhere.

2. Your lead magnet should be targeted towards your ideal customer persona, as discussed in Chapter 3. It should be something that your target audience would be interested in and find valuable.

3. Your lead magnet should be simple and easy to access. It shouldn't require too much time or effort from the potential customer to access.

4. Promote your lead magnet through social media, email marketing, and other channels to increase visibility and drive traffic to your website.

5. Once you have collected a potential customer's email address through your lead magnet, follow up with an email nurture campaign. This series of automated emails

should provide further value and build a relationship with the potential customer, ultimately moving them towards conversion.

So, how to do it? These are just a few examples of lead magnets that you can create to entice potential customers to sign up for your email list and enter your funnel. The key is to offer something that provides value and is relevant to your target audience.

E-book: Create an informative e-book related to your niche and offer it as a lead magnet. For example, if you're in the fitness industry, you could create an e-book on healthy eating or a guide to a workout routine.

Webinar: Host a free webinar and offer it as a lead magnet to those who sign up. Choose a topic that your target audience is interested in and make the webinar informative and engaging.

Free trial: Offer a free trial of your product or service to entice potential customers to sign up. This can be especially effective for software or subscription-based services.

Checklist: Create a helpful checklist related to your niche and offer it as a lead magnet. For example, if you're in the marketing industry, you could create a checklist for creating effective ad copy.

Quiz or assessment: Create a quiz or assessment related to your product or service and offer it as a lead magnet. This can be a fun and interactive way for potential customers to learn more about your offering.

Template or tool: Create a useful template or tool related to your niche and offer it as a lead magnet. For example, if you're in the graphic design industry, you could create a template for designing a logo, provide a free guide to skincare routines or a printable makeup tutorial if you are in the Beauty industry or provide a free template for creating a marketing plan, or a guide to effective social media advertising if you are into Marketing.

White paper: Create a detailed white paper related to your industry and offer it as a lead magnet. This can be a great way to position yourself as an authority and provide valuable insights to potential customers.

By creating effective lead magnets and following up with targeted email nurture campaigns, you can generate leads and build a strong email list for your business. This will ultimately lead to increased conversions and revenue.

Chapter 6: Understanding the Buyer's Journey

To effectively move potential customers through the funnel and towards conversion, it's important to understand the buyer's journey. The buyer's journey is the process that potential customers go through from initial awareness of a product or service to making a purchase.

The buyer's journey typically consists of three stages:

Awareness Stage

In the awareness stage, potential customers become aware of a problem or need that they have, but they may not yet be aware of your brand or the solutions you offer. The goal of your marketing efforts during this stage is to create awareness and get your brand in front of your target audience.

To create awareness, you can use a variety of tactics such as social media marketing, content marketing, influencer marketing, search engine optimization (SEO), pay-per-click advertising (PPC), and more. The key is to use tactics that align with your target audience's preferences and behaviour. For example, if your target audience is active on Instagram, then Instagram marketing may be a good fit.

To create content that resonates with your audience, you need to understand their pain points, challenges, and interests. In the awareness stage, your content should focus on educating your audience about their problem or need and how your brand can help. By conducting market research and building buyer personas, you can gain a deeper understanding of your audience and create content that speaks directly to them. Do it creating blog posts, social media posts, videos, infographics...

It's important to note that during this stage, you're not trying to sell anything yet. Your goal is simply to get your brand in front of your target audience and establish yourself as a trusted source of information in your industry. By doing so, you increase the chances that potential customers will remember your brand when they're ready to move on to the next stage of the buyer's journey.

Consideration Stage.

The consideration stage is the second stage of the buyer's journey, where potential customers have already become aware of your product or service and are now actively considering whether to make a purchase. At this stage, they are evaluating different options and comparing them based on features, benefits, and price.

As a marketer, your goal in the consideration stage is to provide potential customers with the information they need to make an informed decision. This could include offering free trials, demos, or consultations, providing detailed product specifications and comparisons, and highlighting customer reviews and testimonials.

In addition, it's important to address any potential objections or concerns that potential customers may have about your product or service. This could involve creating content that addresses common questions or providing access to customer support to answer any specific queries.

By providing a positive and informative experience during the consideration stage, you can build trust with potential customers and increase the likelihood that they will ultimately make a purchase from you.

Decision

The third stage of the buyer's journey is the decision stage. At this point, the buyer has identified their problem or need and has evaluated potential solutions. In this stage, they are ready to make a purchase decision and become a customer.

As a marketer, your goal in this stage is to make the buyer's decision as easy as possible. You want to remove any obstacles or doubts they may have and provide them with the information they need to make a confident purchase.

To do this, you can offer a range of resources such as product demos, free trials, case studies, customer testimonials, and reviews. These resources will help the buyer make an informed decision and feel confident in their purchase.

You should also focus on creating a sense of urgency to encourage the buyer to make a purchase. This can be achieved through limited-time offers, promotions, or special deals. By creating a sense of urgency, you can motivate the buyer to take action and make a purchase sooner rather than later.

Finally, it's important to provide excellent customer service in the decision stage. This includes providing clear communication, addressing any concerns or questions the buyer may have, and ensuring a smooth and easy purchasing process.

Overall, the decision stage is crucial in the buyer's journey as it is the point at which the buyer becomes a customer. By providing the right resources, creating a sense of urgency, and providing excellent customer service, you can make this transition as smooth and easy as possible.

By understanding the buyer's journey and where potential customers are in that journey, you can tailor your marketing messages and strategies to meet their specific needs and interests.

For example, during the awareness stage, you may want to create content that educates potential customers about their problem and positions your product or service as a potential solution. During the consideration stage, you may want to provide more detailed information about your product or service and address common objections or concerns. During the decision stage, you may want to provide pricing information, customer reviews, and other social proof to help potential customers make a final decision.

By understanding and catering to the buyer's journey, you can effectively move potential customers through the funnel and towards conversion.

Chapter 7: Defining Your Unique Selling Proposition (USP)

Your Unique Selling Proposition (USP) is what sets you apart from your competitors and gives your customers a reason to choose your product or service over others. It's a key element in your marketing strategy and can make a significant impact on your conversion rates.

Here are some steps for defining your USP:

Identify Your Competitors

The first step in defining your Unique Selling Proposition (USP) is to identify your competitors. This involves researching other businesses in your industry that offer similar products or services to yours. Take note of their strengths and weaknesses, as well as how they position themselves in the market.

By identifying your competitors, you can gain valuable insights into what works and what doesn't in your industry. This information can be used to differentiate your business from others and to develop a compelling USP that resonates with your target audience.

Some ways to identify your competitors include:

- Searching online for businesses that offer similar products or services.

- Asking your existing customers which other businesses they considered before choosing yours

- Attending industry events and conferences to network and learn about other businesses in your space

- Conducting a competitive analysis to evaluate your competitors' strengths and weaknesses

Once you have a list of your competitors, take the time to analyse their marketing messages, branding, and unique selling propositions. This can help you identify areas where you can differentiate your business and create a USP that stands out in the market.

Understand Your Target Audience

Understanding your target audience is crucial not only for defining your USP but also for developing an effective marketing strategy. In Chapter 3, we mentioned the importance of identifying your target audience and conducting market research to understand their needs, preferences, and pain points. By understanding your target audience, you can tailor your messaging and positioning to appeal to their specific needs and motivations.

When it comes to defining your USP, understanding your target audience is essential because it helps you identify what sets your product or service apart from your competitors in a way that resonates with your target audience. You want to make sure that your USP is not only unique but also relevant and appealing to your target audience.

For example, let's say you are a marketing agency that specializes in social media marketing for small businesses. Your competitors might offer similar services, but by understanding your target audience, you might discover that they are particularly concerned about getting a high return on investment (ROI) for their marketing spend. Based on this insight, you could develop a USP that emphasizes your agency's track record of delivering measurable results and a focus on maximizing ROI for your clients.

By aligning your USP with your target audience's needs and preferences, you can differentiate yourself from your competitors and position yourself as the solution to your target audience's specific pain points.

Determine Your Benefits

Once you have a clear understanding of your competitors and target audience, it's time to determine your unique benefits. Consider the features of your product or service and how they provide value to your target audience. Ask yourself: What makes my product or service stand out from my competitors? What specific benefits can I offer that my competitors can't?

To figure out your benefits, you can conduct surveys or focus groups with your target audience to gather feedback and insights. This can help you identify what your audience values most and how your product or service can meet their needs better than your competitors.

When determining your benefits, it's important to be specific and highlight how your product or service solves a specific problem or meets a specific need for your target audience. This can help differentiate you from your competitors and provide a clear value proposition for potential customers.

Once you have identified your benefits, it's important to communicate them clearly and consistently in all your marketing materials and messaging. This can help build brand awareness and create a strong brand identity that resonates with your target audience.

Identify Your Unique Features

What sets your product or service apart from your competitors? Is there a unique feature or benefit that only you offer? Identifying your unique features is an essential step in defining your USP. It involves understanding what sets your product or service apart from your competitors. Your unique features could be a specific product feature, a unique service offering, or a particular benefit that only you offer.

To identify your unique features, start by reviewing your product or service in comparison to your competitors. Analyse the features and benefits that you offer that are unique or differentiated from what your competitors provide. These could be features or benefits that are not offered by your competitors or those that you excel in delivering.

Another way to identify your unique features is by conducting customer research. Ask your customers what they love about your product or service and what sets it apart from your competitors. Look for common themes and features that are mentioned repeatedly by your customers.

Once you have identified your unique features, incorporate them into your marketing messaging. Highlight these features on your website, in your social media posts, and in your advertising campaigns. Make sure that they are communicated clearly and consistently throughout all your marketing efforts.

By identifying your unique features, you can create a USP that stands out in a crowded market. This will help you attract and retain customers by communicating the value and benefits that you uniquely offer.

Craft Your USP Statement

Crafting a strong USP statement can be challenging, but it is essential for differentiating your business in a crowded marketplace. Your USP statement should be easy to understand and communicate your unique selling proposition in a clear and concise manner. Avoid using industry jargon or buzzwords that may confuse your audience.

Focus on the benefits that your product or service provides to your target audience. Highlight how your offering solves a problem or meets a need that your competitors do not. Consider using emotional appeal to connect with your target audience on a deeper level. For example, if you offer a product that helps people save time, focus on how this benefit will help them spend more time with their families or pursue their passions.

Once you have crafted your USP statement, test it with your target audience to see how they respond. Use their feedback to refine your message and make it more effective.

Here is an example of a USP statement for a marketing agency focused on SEO:

> " At our marketing agency, we don't just get your website to the top of search engine results pages - we drive high-quality traffic that converts. Our team of expert SEO specialists uses proven strategies and innovative techniques to ensure your website ranks for the right keywords and reaches your ideal audience. With our data-driven approach and personalized service, we deliver measurable results that drive growth for your business. "

Test your message

Once you have crafted your USP statement, it is important to test it. You can do this by getting feedback from customers, running A/B tests on your website and marketing materials, and analysing the results. This will help you determine if your message is resonating with your target audience and if there are any areas that need to be improved upon.

For example, you could run a Google AdWords campaign with two different ad copies: one featuring your USP statement and another without it. By tracking the click-through rates and conversion rates of each ad, you can find the effectiveness of your USP statement and adjust accordingly.

Testing your message is an ongoing process that should be done regularly to ensure that your USP remains relevant and effective. As your business evolves and your target audience changes, your USP may need to be refined or completely revamped to stay competitive in the market.

By defining your unique selling proposition, you can differentiate yourself from your competitors and communicate your value to potential customers. This can ultimately lead to increased conversions and revenue for your business.

Chapter 8: Creating Compelling Content for Your Funnel

Effective content is key to moving potential customers through the funnel and towards conversion. Here are some tips for creating compelling content that resonates with your target audience. Understanding your target audience will help you create content that is relevant and valuable to them so we are now in a position to ask two important questions to define our goals: What do we want our content to achieve? Do we want to generate leads, build brand awareness, or drive sales? Defining your goals will help you create content that is tailored to your desired outcomes.

The first question you need to solve is the format you want to use. When choosing the right format for your content, it's important to consider your message and target audience. Are you trying to convey complex information or emotional storytelling? Are your target audience more likely to engage with written or visual content? Once you have a clear understanding of your message and audience, you can choose the format that best suits your needs. There are many different formats for content, including blog posts, videos, infographics, and more.

For example, if you are trying to explain a complicated concept or provide in-depth analysis, a blog post or whitepaper might be the best format. On the other hand, if you want to create a more emotional connection with your audience, a video or podcast might be more effective. If you want to grab your audience's attention quickly and visually, an infographic or social media graphic might be the way to go.

Ultimately, the goal is to choose a format that will resonate with your audience and effectively convey your message. Don't be afraid to experiment with different formats to see what works best for your brand and audience.

Your content should provide real value to your target audience. It should solve a problem, answer a question, or provide useful information to your audience. Your content should also align with your overall marketing strategy and goals, as well as with the needs and interests of your target audience.

When creating content, consider what type of information or solutions your audience is searching for, and how you can provide that information in a way that is engaging and memorable. You should also consider the tone and style of your content, and how it fits with your brand image and voice.

One effective approach is to use storytelling to connect with your audience on a deeper level. This can involve sharing personal experiences, case studies, or customer success stories that illustrate the benefits of your product or service.

Another important factor is to make your content easy to consume and share. This includes formatting your content in a way that is visually appealing, using clear and concise language, and incorporating multimedia elements such as images and videos.

Overall, creating valuable and engaging content is a crucial component of any successful funnel marketing strategy. By providing helpful and informative content, you can attract and retain the attention of your target audience, and ultimately drive conversions and sales.

A call-to-action (CTA) is a critical element in your content marketing strategy as it directs your readers to take the next step towards becoming a customer. Your CTA should be clear and specific, telling your readers what action to take and why it's important. For example, if you're creating a blog post about your new product, your CTA could be to sign up for a free trial or to visit your product page to learn more.

It's essential to make your CTA stand out by using bold text, contrasting colours, or buttons to draw attention to it. Make sure your CTA is visible throughout your content, whether it's at the end of a blog post or in the middle of a video. Your CTA should be relevant to the content and provide value to your readers.

Additionally, consider using different types of CTAs in your content marketing strategy, such as offering a limited-time promotion or providing a free resource in exchange for signing up for your newsletter. The type of CTA you use will depend on the goal of your content and the stage of the buyer's journey your reader is in. By using clear and compelling CTAs, you can increase the likelihood of turning your readers into customers.

Also, you need to optimize your content for search engines. This is crucial for increasing your website's visibility and attracting more traffic. Conduct keyword research to identify the keywords and phrases that your target audience is searching for. Use these keywords naturally throughout your content, including in headings, subheadings, and body text.

Make sure your meta descriptions are compelling and include your target keywords. Meta descriptions are the snippets of text that appear in search engine results below the title. They provide a summary of your content and encourage people to click through to your website.

Are your URLs descriptive and include relevant keywords? For example, instead of using a generic URL like "www.mywebsite.com/page1," use a descriptive URL like "www.mywebsite.com/seo-best-practices."

Use descriptive alt tags and file names for your images and compress them to reduce load times.

Link to other relevant pages on your website within your content. This helps search engines understand the structure of your website and can improve your search rankings.

Optimize your content for search engines, so you can attract more traffic to your website and increase your chances of converting visitors into customers. Also, by sharing your content on platforms like Facebook, Twitter, LinkedIn, and Instagram, you can increase its visibility and drive traffic to your website. But be careful, not all social media platforms are created equal. Each platform has its own unique audience and strengths, so it's important to choose the right platform(s) for your content. For example, if your content is highly visual, platforms like Instagram and Pinterest may be a good fit. Social media is a powerful tool for promoting your content and reaching a wider audience.

The headline of your content is often the first thing people see, so it's important to make it compelling and attention-grabbing. Use action words, numbers, and other techniques to make your headlines stand out. Visual content is more likely to be shared on social media than text-only content. Invest in high-quality images, graphics, and videos to make your content more engaging and shareable.

Hashtags can help your content reach a wider audience on social media. Use relevant hashtags in your posts to increase visibility and encourage engagement. Social media is a two-way street so you must engage with your audience by responding to comments, sharing user-generated content, and starting conversations.

By creating compelling content that provides value to your target audience, incorporates calls-to-action, and is optimized for search engines and social media, you can effectively move potential customers through the funnel and towards conversion.

preferences, and your budget to determine the most suitable format for your lead magnet. Popular formats include eBooks, webinars, checklists, templates, and case studies.

Provide Value

Your lead magnet should provide real value to your target audience. It should offer a solution to a problem, answer a question, or provide useful information. Providing value is crucial for your lead magnet to be effective. Your potential customers should see your lead magnet as something that is worth their time and attention. The more valuable your lead magnet is, the more likely they are to provide their contact information in exchange for it.

Keep It Simple

A lead magnet should be simple and straightforward to consume. The information presented should be easy to understand so that potential customers can quickly engage with the content and move further down the sales funnel. Using bullet points, clear headings, and concise language can help to keep your lead magnet simple and effective..

Include a Strong Call-to-Action (CTA)

A strong call-to-action (CTA) is critical in encouraging potential customers to take the next step in their customer journey. Your lead magnet should include a clear and compelling CTA that tells them exactly what to do next, whether it's signing up for a newsletter, following you on

Chapter 9: Crafting Your Lead Magnet

What is a lead magnet? How does it work? Why is so important to master it? A lead magnet is a valuable piece of content that you offer to potential customers in exchange for their contact information, and it's an effective way to generate leads and move them down the funnel. To create an effective lead magnet, here are the key points to consider:

Understand Your Target Audience

Knowing your target audience is crucial in creating a lead magnet that is relevant and valuable to them. This will ensure that your lead magnet is targeted to the right people. Choosing the right audience for your lead magnet is the first step in creating an effective marketing strategy. Understanding the needs, preferences, and pain points of your target audience will help you create content that resonates with them and provides real value. This will not only improve the chances of converting leads into customers but also help you build a loyal following.

Choose the Right Format

Select the format that aligns with your message and target audience to achieve optimal results. Choosing the right format for your lead magnet is essential to ensure that your message resonates with your target audience. This will increase the chances of your lead magnet being successful in generating leads. Consider factors such as the type of information you want to convey, your audience's social media, or making a purchase. The CTA should be prominent and easy to find, ideally placed at the end of your lead magnet or in a prominent location on the page.

Optimize for Conversions

Optimizing your lead magnet for conversions is crucial to ensure that you are generating leads effectively. One way to optimize for conversions is to make sure that your lead magnet includes a clear and prominent sign-up form that is easy to fill out. This form should be placed in a strategic location on your website or landing page where potential customers can easily see it and access it. It's also essential to test different headlines and designs for your lead magnet to see which ones are the most effective at converting leads. You can use A/B testing to experiment with different versions of your lead magnet and track the results to see which version performs best. You should track metrics such as the number of sign-ups, conversion rates, and engagement rates to gain insights into how your lead magnet is performing. By regularly monitoring these metrics, you can make data-driven decisions on how to improve your lead magnet to maximize its conversion potential.

In conclusion, crafting an effective lead magnet is an essential component of your marketing strategy. By following the steps outlined in this chapter and continuously optimizing your lead magnet, you can generate leads, build trust and credibility with your target audience, and move potential customers further down the funnel.

Chapter 10: Building Your Landing Page

Your landing page is a critical part of your funnel, as it's the page where potential customers land after clicking on your ad or other marketing efforts. Therefore, it's essential to ensure that your landing page is well-designed and optimized for conversions. But, how to build an effective landing page?

What do you want your landing page to achieve? Do you want to generate leads, build brand awareness, or drive sales? Defining your goals will help you create a landing page that is tailored to your desired outcomes.

- Your landing page should be simple and easy to navigate, with a clear and concise message. Avoid clutter and unnecessary information that can distract potential customers from your message. Keep it simple.

- Your headline should be attention-grabbing and clearly communicate the value proposition of your offering. Including a strong headline will help you.

- Your landing page should provide real value to potential customers, with a clear and compelling offer. This could be a free trial, a discount, or other incentive to encourage them to act. People love free stuff, so take advantage of it and get something in exchange (upsell your product, signing up for your newsletter, joining your Social Media group...)

- High-quality visuals, such as images and videos, can help convey your message and make your landing page more engaging. A picture is worth thousand words.

- Incorporate social proof, such as customer testimonials or reviews, to build credibility and trust with potential customers.

- Every landing page should include a clear and prominent call-to-action (CTA) that encourages potential customers to take a specific action, such as making a purchase or signing up for a newsletter.

- Make sure your landing page is optimized for conversions by testing different headlines, designs, and CTAs, and tracking your results.

In summary, building a high-converting landing page is an essential part of your marketing strategy. It is a page where potential customers land after clicking on your ad or other marketing efforts, and it's the first point of contact between you and your potential customers. By creating a landing page that is simple, provides value, includes social proof, and is optimized for conversions, you can effectively move potential customers through the funnel and towards conversion. Make sure to test different elements of your landing page, track your results, and make necessary adjustments to improve its performance. With a well crafted landing page you can increase your conversion rates and achieve your marketing goals easily.

Chapter 11: Optimizing Your Thank You Page

When someone fills out a form or makes a purchase, they are expressing interest in your product or service, and the thank you page is an opportunity to reinforce that interest and move them closer to becoming a loyal customer. The thank you page should provide clear and concise information on what happens next, whether it's a confirmation email or a download link. Additionally, you can include social sharing buttons or links to related content to keep the potential customer engaged and encourage them to share your message with others. A well-designed thank you page can help build trust with your audience, reinforce your brand messaging, and increase the likelihood of future conversions.

So, how do we build a Thank You page?

First of all, your thank you page should express gratitude to potential customers for taking the desired action. This can help build a positive relationship with them and increase the likelihood of future conversions. It is an opportunity to provide additional value to potential customers. This could include offering additional resources, providing relevant content, or recommending related products or services. When a potential customer takes a desired action, such as filling out a form or making a purchase, your thank you page should convey genuine appreciation for their action. By expressing gratitude, you can build a positive relationship preferences, and your budget to determine the most suitable format for your lead magnet. Popular formats include eBooks, webinars, checklists, templates, and case studies.

Provide Value

Your lead magnet should provide real value to your target audience. It should offer a solution to a problem, answer a question, or provide useful information. Providing value is crucial for your lead magnet to be effective. Your potential customers should see your lead magnet as something that is worth their time and attention. The more valuable your lead magnet is, the more likely they are to provide their contact information in exchange for it.

Keep It Simple

A lead magnet should be simple and straightforward to consume. The information presented should be easy to understand so that potential customers can quickly engage with the content and move further down the sales funnel. Using bullet points, clear headings, and concise language can help to keep your lead magnet simple and effective..

Include a Strong Call-to-Action (CTA)

A strong call-to-action (CTA) is critical in encouraging potential customers to take the next step in their customer journey. Your lead magnet should include a clear and compelling CTA that tells them exactly what to do next, whether it's signing up for a newsletter, following you on

Chapter 9: Crafting Your Lead Magnet

What is a lead magnet? How does it work? Why is so important to master it? A lead magnet is a valuable piece of content that you offer to potential customers in exchange for their contact information, and it's an effective way to generate leads and move them down the funnel. To create an effective lead magnet, here are the key points to consider:

Understand Your Target Audience

Knowing your target audience is crucial in creating a lead magnet that is relevant and valuable to them. This will ensure that your lead magnet is targeted to the right people. Choosing the right audience for your lead magnet is the first step in creating an effective marketing strategy. Understanding the needs, preferences, and pain points of your target audience will help you create content that resonates with them and provides real value. This will not only improve the chances of converting leads into customers but also help you build a loyal following.

Choose the Right Format

Select the format that aligns with your message and target audience to achieve optimal results. Choosing the right format for your lead magnet is essential to ensure that your message resonates with your target audience. This will increase the chances of your lead magnet being successful in generating leads. Consider factors such as the type of information you want to convey, your audience's with potential customers and increase the chances of future conversions. Additionally, the thank you page presents an opportunity to provide additional value to potential customers. You can use this page to offer them extra resources, such as free guides or tutorials, or provide relevant content that they may find useful. You can also recommend related products or services that may interest them. This way, you can further engage with potential customers and encourage them to continue their journey through your funnel.

Encouraging potential customers to share their experience with others can be a powerful way to increase brand awareness and generate additional leads. Your thank you page can play an important role in this process by providing social sharing buttons or other tools that make it easy for them to share your message on social media. By doing so, you can amplify your message and reach a wider audience, potentially attracting new leads and customers. To make it more effective, you can also incentivize them to share by offering discounts or other rewards for referrals. This can motivate them to spread the word about your brand and drive more traffic to your website. Overall, including social sharing buttons on your thank you page can help turn satisfied customers into brand ambassadors, increasing your reach and driving more conversions over time.

A clear and prominent call-to-action (CTA) is a crucial element of your thank you page, as it provides potential customers with the next step to engage with your brand. The CTA should be specific and relevant to the action they just took. For instance, if they just made a purchase, the CTA could be to check their email for a receipt and shipping information. Alternatively, if they just filled out a form, the CTA could be to download an exclusive resource or join a community. Additionally, the CTA should be visually distinct and stand out on the page to ensure it is easily noticeable. By including a clear and prominent CTA, you increase the chances of converting potential customers into loyal customers.

Finally, it's crucial to optimize your thank you page for conversions by continuously testing different headlines, designs, and CTAs, and monitoring your results. Don't hesitate to keep testing until you achieve the desired outcomes. You can effectively move potential customers through the funnel and towards conversion with your Thank you page.

Chapter 12: The importance of your sales page

Your sales page is a critical component of your funnel as it's the page that has the potential to convert potential customers into paying customers. This page should provide all the information potential customers need to make an informed decision about your product or service and persuade them to take the desired action - whether that be making a purchase or signing up for a free trial. Keep the page simple tho. Avoid clutter and unnecessary information that can distract potential customers from your message.

Use a clear and compelling headline that clearly communicates the key benefit of your product or service and grabs the attention of potential customers to encourage them to keep reading. The sales page should highlight the key features and benefits of your product or service, and how it can solve the problems or meet the needs of potential customers. Use clear and concise language, and avoid using industry jargon that could be confusing. Make sure to include images and videos that showcase your product or service to help convey your message and make your sales page more engaging, and provide social proof in the form of customer testimonials or case studies , to build credibility and trust with potential customers.

It's also important to make the purchasing process as easy and straightforward as possible. Include a prominent and clear call-to-action that directs potential customers to the next step in the purchasing process. Use language that creates a sense of urgency, such as limited time offers or limited stock availability, to encourage potential customers to take action.

Finally, like all other parts of your funnel, it's important to optimize your sales page for conversions. Test different headlines, designs, and calls-to-action to determine what works best for your audience, and use data to inform your decisions. By continually testing and refining your sales page, you can increase the likelihood of converting potential customers into paying customers.

By designing an effective sales page that is simple, focused, provides clear and concise information, uses high-quality visuals, addresses potential objections, includes social proof, includes a clear call-to-action, and is optimized for conversions, you can effectively move potential customers through the funnel and towards conversion.

Chapter 13: Implementing Effective Call-to-Actions.

In today's digital age, it's more important than ever for businesses to have a strong online presence to attract potential customers and generate leads. One of the key elements in achieving this goal is by creating a well-designed funnel, which guides potential customers through a series of steps towards a desired conversion. However, even the best funnel can fall short without effective call-to-actions (CTAs).

CTAs are crucial elements in any funnel, as they guide and prompt potential customers to take a specific action, such as making a purchase or subscribing to a newsletter. They are the final step in converting leads into customers and can significantly impact the success of your funnel.

Creating effective can be a challenging and time-consuming task that requires testing and experimentation with different options. It may take some time and effort to find the best approach that resonates with your audience and prompts them to take the desired action. However, by persistently testing and refining your CTAs, you can optimize your funnel for conversions and increase the likelihood of success.

There are several tips and best practices that can make the process of creating effective CTAs easier. Firstly, your CIA should be clear and specific about the action you want potential customers to take. You need to use action-oriented language that is easy to understand and encourages potential customers to act. This could be as simple as using phrases such as "Sign Up Now" or "Buy Today." Avoid vague or ambiguous language that could confuse potential customers.

In addition to clear and specific language, it is important to make your CTA stand out from the rest of the content on your page. This can be achieved using contrast and visual hierarchy. Using a different color, font, or size can help make your CTA more visually prominent and easily distinguishable from other elements on your page. This will help draw attention to your CTA and make it more likely that potential customers will take action.

Another important consideration when implementing CTAs is their strategic placement. Your CTA should be easy to find and accessible to potential customers. Consider placing it above the fold or in multiple locations throughout your funnel to ensure that potential customers have multiple opportunities to take action.

Creating a sense of urgency or scarcity can also be an effective way to encourage potential customers to take action. By using language that conveys the importance of acting now, such as "Limited Time Offer" or "Only X Spots Left," you can create a sense of urgency and scarcity that motivates potential customers to act quickly so they take action before it's too late.

Testing different CTAs is also an important part of the process. Experiment with different wording, colors, and placement to find the most effective combination for your audience. Use data and analytics to optimize your CTAs over time. Track your conversion rates and make changes to your

CTAs as needed to improve your results. This will help you identify the CTAs that generate the most conversions and optimize your funnel accordingly.

Implementing effective CTAs can be a challenging task, but it is crucial for the success of your funnel marketing strategy. By keeping in mind the tips and best practices outlined above, you can create more compelling and persuasive CTAs that drive potential customers to take the desired action.

Remember that testing and experimenting with different options is key to finding what works best for your specific audience and business goals. It may take some time and effort to master the art of creating effective CTAs, but the potential payoff in terms of increased conversions and revenue is well worth it.

Don't be afraid to continue tweaking and optimizing your CTAs over time as you gather more data and insights on what works best for your business. By continuously refining and improving your CTAs, you can ensure that your funnel marketing strategy remains effective and successful in driving conversions and growing your business.

Chapter 14: Creating a Sense of Urgency

Creating a sense of urgency is an effective marketing technique that can greatly impact the success of your funnel. It can motivate potential customers to take immediate action, resulting in more conversions and revenue for your business. Urgency triggers a psychological response in customers that drives them to act sooner rather than later, as they fear missing out on an opportunity. By utilizing this technique, you can make your offers more compelling and drive more sales. Creating urgency can be especially important for time-sensitive promotions or limited-time offers, where a sense of scarcity can further increase the likelihood of a sale. In the following sections, we will explore some practical strategies and best practices to help you effectively create urgency in your funnel and drive more conversions.

Here are some ways to create a sense of urgency in your funnel:

Limited Time Offers

Limited time offers can be an incredibly effective way to create a sense of urgency and drive sales in your business. When potential customers are faced with a time limit or deadline, they are more likely to act quickly to take advantage of the offer before it expires. This can be especially effective for customers who are already interested in your product or service but may need an extra push to make a purchase.

To create an effective limited time offer, it is important to think carefully about the specifics of the offer. Consider what type of discount or bonus you want to offer and for how long the offer will be available. You may want to offer a percentage discount off the regular price, a free gift with purchase, or a special bundle deal.

It's also important to think about how you will promote the limited time offer. You can use various channels such as email marketing, social media, or paid advertising to communicate the urgency of the offer and encourage customers to take advantage of it before it expires. Make sure to clearly communicate the terms and expiration date of the offer, as well as any restrictions or limitations that may apply.

Keep in mind that while limited time offers can be effective, they should not be used too frequently or in a way that undermines the perceived value of your product or service. Make sure that the offer aligns with your overall brand and marketing strategy and that it is something that will genuinely resonate with your target audience. With careful planning and execution, limited time offers can be a powerful tool for creating a sense of urgency and driving sales in your business.

Scarcity

Scarcity is a psychological principle that is based on the idea that people value things more when they are rare or in short supply. When potential customers believe that a product or service is scarce or limited, they are more likely to take action quickly to avoid missing out on the opportunity.

There are different ways to create a sense of scarcity. One common approach is to limit the availability of your product or service. For example, you could create a limited edition version of your product or offer a service that is only available for a certain period. By making your product or service appear exclusive or rare, potential customers may feel more motivated to take action quickly.

Another way to create scarcity is by communicating that there is a limited supply of your product or service. This approach can be particularly effective for products or services that are in high demand. For example, you could use language on your sales page such as "only X items left in stock" or "limited quantities available." By creating a sense of urgency around the availability of your product or service, potential customers may feel more motivated to make a purchase before it's too late.

It's important to use scarcity ethically and transparently. If you create a false sense of scarcity, potential customers may feel misled or lose trust in your business. Additionally, using scarcity too frequently or in a manipulative way can also have a negative impact on your business's reputation. By using scarcity judiciously and honestly, you can create a sense of urgency that motivates potential customers to take action while maintaining trust and credibility.

Countdown Timers

Countdown timers can be an effective tool for creating a sense of urgency on your landing pages or sales pages. When potential customers see a countdown timer, it creates a visual representation of time ticking away, adding a sense of scarcity to your offer. This scarcity can trigger a psychological response that compels people to take action before it's too late.

The use of countdown timers can be especially effective when you're running a limited-time promotion or sale. By highlighting that there's only a certain amount of time left to take advantage of the offer, you can motivate potential customers to take action and make a purchase.

Additionally, countdown timers can help to increase customer engagement and reduce bounce rates. By creating a sense of urgency and prompting potential customers to take action, they are less likely to leave your page without taking any action.

It's important to note that while countdown timers can be an effective tool, they should be used judiciously. Overuse of countdown timers can diminish their effectiveness and even create a sense of distrust with your potential customers. To maximize their impact, countdown timers should be used strategically and sparingly, and always with a clear and compelling call-to-action.

Personalization

Personalization in marketing refers to tailoring the content and messaging of your marketing campaigns to the specific interests, preferences, and behaviors of your target audience. By personalizing your marketing messages, you can create a stronger connection with your potential customers, making them more likely to engage with your brand and take action.

One way to use personalization to create a sense of urgency is by making potential customers feel like the offer is tailored specifically to them. For example, you can use data on their past purchases, browsing history, or demographics to customize your messaging and offers. By doing this, you can create a sense of exclusivity and make potential customers feel like they are receiving a special offer that is only available to them.

Another way to use personalization to create a sense of urgency is by using targeted messaging and dynamic content. For example, you can use geolocation data to show potential customers how much time is left for a sale or promotion in their local time zone. By displaying this information in real-time, you can create a sense of urgency and encourage potential customers to take action before it's too late.

Personalization can also be used in email marketing campaigns to create a sense of urgency. By using personalized subject lines and email content that is tailored to the recipient's interests and preferences, you can increase the chances that they will open and engage with your emails. You can also use personalization to send targeted emails to specific segments of your audience, such as those who have abandoned their shopping carts or those who have not made a purchase in a while.

Overall, personalizing your marketing messages can be an effective way to create a sense of urgency and encourage potential customers to take action. By using data and targeted messaging, you can make potential customers feel like the offer is specifically for them, and create a sense of exclusivity that can increase the likelihood of a sale.

Social Proof

Social proof is a powerful tool in marketing and can be particularly effective in creating a sense of urgency. By using customer reviews or testimonials on your sales page or in your marketing materials, you can demonstrate to potential customers that others have already taken advantage of your offer and had a positive experience. This can be particularly effective in situations where potential customers may be hesitant or skeptical, as seeing positive reviews from others can help to build trust and credibility.

There are several different ways to use social proof to create a sense of urgency. One approach is to include customer reviews or testimonials that highlight the benefits of your product or service and emphasize the positive outcomes that others have experienced. This can be particularly effective when potential customers are in the later stages of the funnel and are actively considering making a purchase.

Another approach is to highlight the popularity or demand for your product or service. This can be done by including statements such as "Limited Stock Remaining" or "Only a Few Spots Left" to create a sense of urgency and encourage potential customers to act quickly. By highlighting the scarcity of your offer, you can create a sense of urgency and increase the likelihood of a sale.

Ultimately, the key to using social proof effectively to create a sense of urgency is to be authentic and genuine. It is important to only use reviews or testimonials that are honest and accurate, and to avoid exaggerating or misrepresenting the experiences of others. By using social proof in a responsible and ethical manner, you can create a sense of urgency that encourages potential customers to take action and move through the funnel towards conversion.

Emphasize the Consequences of Inaction

When it comes to creating a sense of urgency, emphasizing the consequences of inaction is a powerful tool in your marketing arsenal. By making potential customers aware of what they stand to lose if they don't act quickly, you can increase their motivation to take action and move them closer to conversion.

One way to emphasize the consequences of inaction is to communicate the potential negative outcomes of not taking action. For instance, you can communicate that the price of the product or service will increase, which can encourage potential customers to act now and avoid paying more later. Another approach is to highlight that the offer is limited or has an expiration date, which creates a sense of scarcity and urgency.

In addition to highlighting the negative consequences of inaction, you can also emphasize the positive outcomes of taking action. For example, you can highlight the benefits that potential customers will gain by acting now, such as access to exclusive content or a special discount. This can create a sense of excitement and anticipation that motivates potential customers to take action.

Another effective way to create a sense of urgency is to use time-sensitive language in your CTAs. For instance, you can use phrases like "Limited time offer" or "Act now before it's too late" to create a sense of urgency and encourage potential customers to act quickly.

Overall, emphasizing the consequences of inaction is a powerful technique for creating a sense of urgency in your marketing efforts. By highlighting the potential negative outcomes of not acting and emphasizing the positive benefits of acting now, you can increase the motivation of potential customers and move them closer to conversion.

In conclusion, incorporating a sense of urgency into your funnel can be a powerful technique to increase conversions and drive revenue for your business. By leveraging various tactics such as limited time offers, scarcity, countdown timers, personalization, social proof, and emphasizing the consequences of inaction, you can effectively create urgency and prompt potential customers to take action. Keep in mind that each tactic may work differently for different audiences, so it's important to test and analyze the results to find the most effective combination for your business. By continuously refining your approach and incorporating a sense of urgency into your funnel, you can encourage more potential customers to convert and ultimately boost your bottom line. Hard work pays off!

Chapter 15: Using Social Proof to Boost Conversions

As we discussed earlier, social proof can be a game-changer when it comes to increasing conversions in your funnel. Essentially, social proof is the phenomenon where people are more likely to take action or make a decision based on the actions or opinions of others. When potential customers see that others are already engaging with your product or service, they are more likely to do the same. So, it's important to include social proof in your funnel strategy but it's important to use it ethically and authentically. Don't fake reviews or endorsements, as this can ultimately damage your reputation and turn potential customers away. Instead, focus on providing an excellent product or service that speaks for itself, and encourage satisfied customers to share their experiences. With the right approach, social proof can be a valuable asset to your funnel and help boost conversions.

Customer Reviews and testimonials

Including customer reviews or testimonials on your landing pages and sales pages can be a powerful form of social proof. Positive reviews can serve as testimonials to your product or service, building trust and credibility with potential customers. This trust can translate into increased conversions as customers are more likely to make a purchase when they feel that others have had positive experiences with your brand.

One effective way to incorporate this is to feature them prominently on your landing pages and sales pages. This allows potential customers to easily access them and see what others have to say about your product or service. You can also use customer reviews as part of your retargeting and email marketing campaigns to further reinforce the positive experiences of existing customers.

By incorporating customer reviews, testimonials, you can leverage the power of social proof to increase conversions in your funnel. Not only do they help build trust and credibility, but they also provide valuable feedback for improving your product or service.

Case Studies

Case studies can be an effective form of social proof because they provide potential customers with a detailed and specific look at how your product or service has helped others. By showcasing real-world examples of how your product or service has solved problems or met the needs of previous customers, you can instil confidence and trust in new prospects.

When creating case studies, it's important to choose examples that highlight the most impressive results or outcomes achieved by previous customers. The case study should be well-written and easy to understand, using clear and concise language to explain how your product or service was used and what the specific results were. Including quotes or testimonials from the customer can add an extra layer of credibility and help to reinforce the benefits of your product or service.

It's also important to ensure that the case study is relevant to your target audience. For example, if your product or service is aimed at a specific industry or niche, choose a case study that showcases how your product or service helped a customer in that industry or niche. This will make it easier for potential customers to see how your product or service could benefit them specifically.

By including well-crafted case studies as part of your social proof strategy, you can build trust and credibility with potential customers, increasing the likelihood that they will convert and become loyal customers.

Influencer Endorsements

Partnering with influencers can be an effective way to leverage social proof in your funnel. If you have influencers in your niche or industry, consider collaborating with them to promote your product or service. When an influencer endorses your product or service, it can create a sense of trust and social proof among their followers, increasing the likelihood of a sale.

Another way to incorporate social proof in your funnel is to feature influencers or thought leaders in your industry who have used and endorsed your product or service. This type of social proof can help build authority and establish your brand as a leader in your field. For instance, if you sell a fitness product, you could feature a well-known fitness influencer who has used and recommended your product. This can not only increase your credibility but also attract potential customers who trust the influencer's opinion.

By partnering with influencers, featuring thought leaders, and leveraging customer reviews, you can establish your brand as a trustworthy and reliable choice for potential customers.

Social Media Engagement.

Social media has become an integral part of our daily lives, and businesses have taken advantage of this by using it as a platform to build their brand and connect with potential customers. One way to use social media to increase conversions in your funnel is by leveraging social proof. Social proof can come in many forms, including engagement on social media. This engagement can take the form of likes, shares, and comments on your social media posts.

When potential customers see others engaging with your brand on social media, it can have a powerful effect on building trust and credibility. It shows that real people are using and enjoying your product or service, which can encourage others to do the same. This form of social proof can be especially effective when it comes to younger demographics who are more likely to turn to social media for recommendations and reviews.

To take advantage of this type of social proof, be sure to promote your social media presence across all of your marketing channels. Encourage customers to engage with your brand by including calls to action in your social media posts, such as asking them to share their experiences or leave reviews. Responding to comments and engaging with your audience on social media can also help to build trust and foster a sense of community around your brand.

Overall, using social proof in the form of engagement on social media can be a powerful tool in increasing conversions in your funnel. By leveraging the influence of others and building trust and credibility with potential customers, you can encourage them to take action and move through the funnel towards conversion.

User Generated Content

Encouraging user-generated content is a highly effective way to create social proof in your funnel. By asking your customers to share photos or videos of themselves using your product or service, you can showcase real-life examples of how your offerings can benefit others. Seeing happy and satisfied customers is a powerful motivator for potential customers, as it creates a sense of trust and authenticity around your brand.

User-generated content also helps to build a community around your brand, which can increase engagement with potential customers. When people see that others are using and enjoying your product or service, they may feel more inclined to engage with your brand themselves. This can lead to increased website traffic, social media engagement, and ultimately, more conversions.

To encourage user-generated content, consider running a social media contest or offering incentives for customers who share photos or videos of themselves using your product or service. You can also feature user-generated content on your website and social media channels to showcase the positive experiences of your customers. By leveraging the power of social proof through user-generated content, you can boost conversions in your funnel and build a strong community around your brand.

In conclusion, by using social proof in your funnel, you can build trust and credibility with potential customers, which can ultimately lead to increased conversions and revenue. By incorporating customer reviews, testimonials, case studies, influencer endorsements, social media engagement, and user-generated content into your funnel, you can create a powerful and effective marketing strategy that will help your business succeed.

Chapter 16: Adding Upsells and Downsells to Your Funnel

Upsells and downsells are a popular tactic in modern marketing strategies. Upsells refer to the offering of additional products or services after a customer has made a purchase, while downsells are offered when a customer declines an initial offer. This technique can greatly increase revenue and maximize the value of each customer.

Upselling is a great way to increase revenue as it allows you to offer customers complementary products that they may be interested in. For example, if a customer has purchased a laptop, you can offer them accessories such as a protective case or a mouse. By offering upsells, you are providing additional value to the customer and increasing the chances of them making another purchase.

However, it's important to note that upselling should be done with the customer's best interest in mind. Pushing unnecessary or irrelevant products may result in a negative experience for the customer and harm your brand reputation. Instead, focus on offering products that will enhance the customer's experience and provide them with additional value.

Downselling, on the other hand, is a technique used to save a sale that would otherwise be lost. For example, if a customer declines an initial offer, you can offer them a lower-priced alternative instead of losing the sale altogether. This can be a win-win situation as the customer may still make a purchase, and you still generate revenue.

To successfully implement downselling, it's important to understand the customer's needs and preferences. Offering an alternative product that is similar in value and benefits to the initial offer can increase the likelihood of the customer making a purchase. However, it's important to not appear pushy or aggressive in your approach as this may deter the customer from making any purchase at all.

When adding upsells and downsells to your funnel, it's important to ensure that the customer journey is smooth and seamless. Offer upsells and downsells at the appropriate stages of the funnel, and ensure that they are relevant to the customer's needs and preferences. For example, offering a complementary product after a customer has made a purchase can increase the chances of them making another purchase, while offering a lower-priced alternative when a customer declines an initial offer can save the sale.

It's also important to communicate the benefits of the upsell or downsell clearly to the customer. Highlight the additional value they will receive by accepting the offer and ensure that they understand the benefits of the product or service. This can increase the likelihood of the customer accepting the offer and making a purchase.

To maximize the effectiveness of upsells and downsells, it's important to test and experiment with different offers and strategies. Analyze the results and make changes as needed to ensure that you are offering the best possible value to your customers.

Upsells and downsells are a powerful technique for increasing revenue and maximizing the value of each customer. When implemented correctly, they can enhance the customer experience and provide additional value. However, it's important to ensure that upsells and downsells are offered with the customer's best interest in mind, and that the customer journey is smooth and seamless. With the right approach and strategy, upsells and downsells can be a valuable addition to your funnel and greatly increase revenue for your business.

Offer Relevant Products or Services

When offering upsells or downsells, make sure that the products or services are relevant to the customer's initial purchase. For example, if a customer has just purchased a software program, you could offer an upsell for a premium version with additional features that would enhance their experience with the software. Upsells should be presented as an opportunity to upgrade and get more value, while downsells should be positioned as a way to still get value even if the initial offer was not a fit for the customer.

Keep Prices Reasonable

Make sure that your upsells and downsells are priced appropriately. Upsells should offer additional value, but the price should still be reasonable. Downsells should be priced lower than the initial offer, but still provide value. You can also consider offering a payment plan option to make the offer more affordable and accessible to customers.

Highlight the Benefits

When it comes to offering upsells or downsells in your funnel, it's important to communicate the benefits that customers will receive. This can be done by highlighting how the additional product or service will enhance their experience or provide additional value.

First, consider the specific benefits of the upsell or downsell. What problem will it solve for the customer? What additional features or capabilities does it offer? Make sure to clearly communicate these benefits in your messaging.

For example, if you're offering an upsell for a premium version of your software, highlight the additional features and functionality that the customer will receive. Maybe the premium version offers more customization options, or includes advanced analytics tools. Emphasize how these features will help the customer achieve their goals or streamline their workflow.

Similarly, if you're offering a downsell after a customer declines an initial offer, explain how the downsell can still meet their needs or solve their problem. Maybe the downsell offers fewer features or a more basic version of the product, but at a lower price point. Highlight the benefits of this option, such as affordability or simplicity.

Time Your Offers Appropriately

Make sure that your upsell and downsell offers are timed appropriately. Upsells should be offered after a customer has made a purchase and is already in a buying mindset.

Downsells should be offered when a customer has declined an initial offer, but is still interested in your product or service. The offer should be presented at the appropriate point in the funnel when the customer is most receptive to it. Going back to the example of an upsell offer for a premium version of a software program may be best presented after the customer has successfully completed the initial purchase and is viewing the confirmation page. On the other hand, if a customer declines an initial offer, it may be because it doesn't align with their specific needs or preferences. Offering a downsell that addresses those needs or preferences can be a more effective way to keep the customer engaged and increase the likelihood of a future purchase.

Use Visuals

In addition to communicating the benefits, it's also important to make the upsell or downsell offer clear and easy to understand. Use clear and concise messaging that clearly explains the offer and the benefits. Use persuasive language that encourages the customer to take action and upgrade to the upsell or accept the downsell and provide visual aids, such as images or videos, that show the upsell or downsell in action. This can help the customer visualize how the additional product or service will enhance their experience.

Using visuals, such as product images or videos, help customers visualize the additional value that your upsell or downsell offers. This can make the offer more enticing and increase the likelihood of a sale.

A/B Test Your Offers

A/B testing is an effective way to optimize your upsell and downsell offers in your funnel. When conducting A/B testing for upsells and downsells, it's important to test different variables such as the products or services being offered, pricing, and timing. For example, you could test offering a higher-priced upsell versus a lower-priced upsell to see which option generates more revenue. Or you could test offering an upsell immediately after the initial purchase versus waiting a certain amount of time to offer the upsell.

To conduct an A/B test, you can create two different variations of your upsell or downsell offers and direct traffic to each version of the offer. You can then track the results and compare the conversion rates and revenue generated by each variation. Some popular tools for A/B testing include Google Optimize, Optimizely, and VWO. When testing different variations of your upsell and downsell offers, it's important to only test one variable at a time to accurately determine which element is contributing to the difference in results. For example, if you're testing different prices for an upsell, you should keep all other elements of the offer the same to accurately determine which price point is most effective.

In conclusion, adding upsells and downsells to your funnel can be a powerful way to increase revenue and maximize the value of each customer. However, it is crucial to approach it strategically and with the customer's needs and preferences in mind. Keep in mind that it's not about pushing irrelevant or unnecessary products, but rather offering relevant and valuable additional products or services at the right time and in a compelling way that enhances the customer's overall experience.

It's important to test different offers and messaging to see what works best for your audience, as well as to ensure that the additional offers do not overshadow the primary offer. Providing clear and concise information about the additional offers can also help customers make informed decisions, and avoiding pushy or aggressive sales tactics can help maintain a positive relationship with customers.

Additionally, it's important to analyze the impact of upsells and downsells on your overall conversion rate and revenue, and make adjustments as necessary. You may find that certain offers or timing work better than others, or that certain products or services have a higher conversion rate when offered as upsells or downsells.

Incorporating upsells and downsells into your funnel is just one of many strategies you can use to increase revenue and customer lifetime value. By focusing on providing a positive customer experience and offering relevant and valuable additional products or services, you can enhance the customer's overall journey and build a loyal customer base that drives long-term success for your business.

Chapter 14: Boosting Your Leads with Email Marketing

Email marketing is a highly effective tool that enables businesses to communicate with their customers and potential clients directly. It is a critical element of any successful funnel as it allows businesses to nurture leads and build strong relationships with their audience. Email marketing is a form of permission-based marketing that allows businesses to connect with their subscribers who have willingly shared their contact information, such as email addresses.

One of the main benefits of email marketing is that it allows you to reach a large audience in a cost-effective way. Compared to other forms of marketing, email marketing has a much higher return on investment (ROI). This is because you are communicating with people who have already expressed an interest in your brand or product, which increases the likelihood of conversion.

Email marketing also enables businesses to segment their audience based on specific demographics or behavior, which allows for targeted messaging. For example, you can segment your audience based on their purchase history, interests, or location, and tailor your emails accordingly. This can increase engagement and improve the effectiveness of your campaigns.

Another benefit of email marketing is that it allows for automation, which can save time and increase efficiency. Automated email campaigns can be triggered by specific actions, such as a sign-up or a purchase, and can include targeted messaging to nurture leads and move them through the funnel.

However, it's essential to keep in mind that email marketing is only effective if it's done correctly. This means that businesses need to provide value to their subscribers and avoid spamming or bombarding their inboxes with irrelevant messages. It's essential to strike a balance between frequency and relevance to keep subscribers engaged and interested.

To make the most of email marketing, it's important to have a clear strategy in place. This includes defining your target audience, setting goals, creating a content plan, and measuring your results. By doing so, you can ensure that your email campaigns are effective, relevant, and provide value to your subscribers.

Here are some ways to use email marketing to feed your leads and build relationships with your audience:

1. ***Provide Valuable Content*** When crafting your email campaigns, focus on providing valuable content to your subscribers. This could include helpful tips, informative articles, or exclusive offers. By providing value, you will establish trust with your audience and keep them engaged.

2. ***Personalize Your Emails*** Personalization is key to building relationships with your subscribers. Use their first name in the email, and tailor the content to their interests and preferences. This will make your emails more relevant and increase the chances of engagement.

3. ***Segment Your List*** Segmenting your email list allows you to send targeted messages to specific groups of subscribers. This could be based on their interests, behaviour, or demographic information. By segmenting your list, you can send more relevant messages and improve your open and click-through rates.

4. ***Use Automation*** Automation allows you to set up email campaigns that are triggered by specific actions or events. For example, you could send a welcome email when someone signs up for your list, a series of educational emails to those who are still learning about your products, or a promotional or follow-up email to those who have already made a purchase. Automation saves time and ensures that your subscribers receive timely and relevant messages.

5. ***Test and Optimize*** A/B testing your email campaigns can help you determine what works best for your audience. Test different subject lines, content, and CTAs to see what resonates with your subscribers. Use the results to optimize your email campaigns and improve your conversion rates.

6. ***Don't Overdo It*** While email marketing is essential, it's important not to overdo it. Bombarding your subscribers with too many emails can lead to unsubscribes or even spam complaints. Find the right frequency for your audience and make sure that each email provides value.

In summary, email marketing is an essential part of any successful funnel. It enables businesses to nurture leads, build strong relationships with their audience, and reach a large audience in a cost-effective way. By segmenting your audience, automating campaigns, and providing value to your subscribers, you can increase engagement and improve the effectiveness of your campaigns. A clear strategy and measurement of results will help you to ensure that your email campaigns are effective and drive revenue for your business.

Chapter 15: How to write a perfect email subject line.

The subject line of your email is critical because it determines whether your subscribers will open your email or not. A great subject line can entice your subscribers to open your email, read your content, and take action. On the other hand, a weak subject line can make your email go unnoticed in your subscribers' inboxes.

To create a compelling subject line, you need to understand your audience and what motivates them. Consider what type of content they find valuable and what problems they are looking to solve. Use language that resonates with them and speaks directly to their needs and desires. Your subject line should clearly convey the purpose of your email in a concise manner. Be clear and concise by avoiding vague or generic subject lines that don't provide any context. Instead, use specific and descriptive language that accurately represents the content of your email and never ever use clickbait or misleading subject lines as they can damage your credibility and trust with your subscribers. Personalization is key to building relationships with your subscribers. Include their name or other personal information in the subject line and you will make the email feel more personal increasing the likelihood of engagement. However, make sure that the personalization is relevant and not intrusive.

Another useful technique for creating a compelling subject line is to create a sense of urgency or curiosity. Using action-oriented language in your subject line can encourage subscribers to take action. Words like "discover," "learn," or "get" can create a sense of excitement and encourage subscribers to open your email. However, make sure that your email content delivers on the promise of the subject line. Also, creating a sense of urgency can motivate subscribers to take action. Words like "limited time" or "last chance" can create a sense of urgency and encourage subscribers to open your email. However, be careful not to overuse this tactic, as it can come across as pushy or manipulative. You could also ask a question or make a bold statement that sparks your subscribers' curiosity and encourages them to open your email.

In addition to making sure your subject line is relevant, it's crucial to keep it concise and attention-grabbing. Email clients typically display only the first 50-60 characters of a subject line, so you need to make those characters count. Your subscribers receive countless emails each day, so you need to make sure your subject line stands out in their inbox. One effective way to make your subject line stand out is to use emojis or symbols. These can add a bit of visual interest to your subject line and help it stand out among the sea of other emails your subscribers receive. However, it's essential to use emojis and symbols in moderation and only if they are relevant to your message.

A few examples of all this for the software company we have been talking before would be:

"Upgrade now and unlock advanced features with our premium version!"

"Experience the full power with our premium version"

"Upgrade to our premium version: More features, more productivity!"

"Ready to take your work to the next level? Try our premium version now!"

"Maximize your potential with our Premium version – upgrade now and save!"

Overall, creating a compelling subject line is crucial for the success of your email marketing campaigns. Take the time to craft subject lines that resonate with your audience, create a sense of urgency or curiosity, and keep them short and to the point. By doing so, you'll increase your open rates and engagement, leading to more conversions and revenue for your business.

By crafting effective email subject lines, you can entice subscribers to open your email and engage with your content. Be clear and concise, create a sense of urgency, personalize your subject line, use action-oriented language, avoid spam trigger words, and test and analyse your subject lines.

Chapter 16: Creating Engaging Email Content

Once you've crafted a compelling subject line, it's time to focus on creating engaging email content that keeps your subscribers interested and motivated to take action. Email marketing is one of the most effective ways to reach and engage with potential customers, build brand awareness, and drive conversions. However, creating an engaging email campaign that resonates with your audience and inspires them to take action can be a challenging task. But with the average person receiving dozens of emails a day, it can be challenging to create email content that stands out and captures your subscribers' attention. It's crucial to create email content that stands out from the crowd and delivers value to your subscribers. By understanding your audience, crafting compelling subject lines, writing engaging email copy, designing visually appealing templates, and testing and measuring your campaigns, you can create email content that resonates with your subscribers and drives conversions.

The key to creating engaging email content is to understand your audience and tailor your messaging to their needs and interests. Take the time to segment your email list based on factors such as demographics, purchase history, and behavior. This allows you to create targeted campaigns that resonate with specific groups of subscribers and improve your overall email engagement rates. By delivering personalized content, you can build stronger relationships with your subscribers and drive higher conversion rates.

Let's explore some of the best practices for creating engaging email content that keeps your subscribers interested and motivated to take action.

Know Your Audience

When it comes to creating engaging email content, one of the most critical factors is understanding your audience. Without a thorough understanding of your subscribers, it can be challenging to create content that resonates with them and drives engagement. Therefore, taking the time to research your subscribers and understand their needs and interests is crucial.

Start by analyzing your subscriber data to gain insights into their behavior, preferences, and demographics. You can use email marketing tools to gather this information, including email opens, clicks, and website visits. Additionally, you can send surveys to your subscribers to get a better understanding of their interests and preferences. With this data, you can segment your subscribers based on their behavior, demographics, or interests, and create targeted email campaigns that speak directly to their needs. This personalized approach can help you create more relevant content that drives engagement and increases conversions.

In addition to segmenting your subscribers, it's essential to create content that is relevant and valuable to them. Your subscribers are busy, and their inboxes are likely inundated with promotional emails. To stand out and keep their attention, you need to create content that provides value and solves their problems. This could be educational content that helps them learn a new skill or informational content that provides insights into industry trends. By providing valuable content, you can build trust with your subscribers and position your brand as a thought leader in your industry. Ultimately, this can help you increase engagement, drive conversions, and grow your business.

Provide Value

Providing value to your subscribers should be a top priority. In today's digital age, people are inundated with emails, and many of them end up in the trash folder without being opened. To make sure your emails stand out from the crowd, you need to provide your subscribers with valuable content that resonates with them.

One way to do this is by offering tips, insights, or exclusive content that they can't find elsewhere. By positioning yourself as a thought leader in your industry, you can establish trust with your subscribers and keep them engaged with your brand. You can also offer solutions to the problems they may be facing or meet their needs by providing them with the information they need to make informed decisions about your products or services.

When you provide value to your subscribers, you are more likely to build long-term relationships with them. This can lead to increased engagement, loyalty, and ultimately, sales. By focusing on the needs of your subscribers and delivering content that is tailored to their interests, you can create a positive perception of your brand and establish yourself as a go-to resource in your industry. In the next section, we'll dive deeper into the strategies you can use to create engaging email content that resonates with your subscribers.

Use Visuals

Visuals can be a game-changer in email marketing. As humans, we are naturally drawn to images and videos, and incorporating them into your emails can help you capture your subscribers' attention and make your content more memorable. High-quality visuals can also make your email content more digestible and easier to understand, especially if you are explaining complex concepts or ideas.

There are many ways to incorporate visuals into your email content. For example, you could use images or graphics to highlight key points, break up text-heavy sections, or add a visual element to a call-to-action. Videos are also an effective way to engage your subscribers, especially if you are demonstrating how to use a product or service or sharing a behind-the-scenes look at your business. However, it's important to make sure that your visuals are relevant to your content and add value to your subscribers' experience.

Keep It Short and Sweet

With the average person receiving dozens, if not hundreds, of emails per day, it's important to make your content easy to digest and understand at a glance. Long paragraphs or dense blocks of text can be overwhelming and may cause your recipients to lose interest quickly. To combat this, it's important to keep your content short and to the point.

Consider breaking up your message into shorter, more easily digestible sections. Use clear and concise language to convey your message, and avoid using jargon or technical terms that may confuse or alienate your readers. By making your content easy to read and understand, you can increase the chances that your recipients will engage with your message and take the desired action. When it comes to crafting engaging email content, brevity is key.

Use a Conversational Tone

Your email content should sound like a conversation between you and your subscriber. You want to create a sense of connection and conversation with them, rather than sounding like a robot sending out automated messages. That's why using a conversational tone in your emails can be so effective. By using language that sounds like a conversation between two people, you can create a more personalized experience for your subscribers. This can help to build trust and rapport with them, which in turn can lead to higher open rates, click-through rates, and ultimately, more conversions. When writing your email content, consider how you would speak to a friend or colleague in person, and try to replicate that tone in your writing.

Include a Call-to-Action

When creating your CTAs, it's important to consider your email's objective and what action you want your subscribers to take. Do you want them to visit your website, sign up for a free trial, or make a purchase? Once you have a clear goal in mind, make sure your CTA is prominent and visible in your email. You could use a button, a link, or a combination of both to make it stand out. Additionally, using action-oriented language in your CTA, such as "Shop now," "Learn more," or "Get started," can help create a sense of urgency and encourage subscribers to take immediate action.

Test and Analyse Your Content

A/B testing is a valuable tool for email marketers to improve the effectiveness of their campaigns. By testing different variables, you can gain insights into what resonates with your audience and refine your approach to maximize engagement and conversion rates. One of the most crucial elements to test is the email content itself, as it can have a significant impact on open and click-through rates.

When testing email content, there are several factors to consider. One is the format of your emails. Do your subscribers respond better to text-only emails, or do they engage more with emails that include images or videos? You can also experiment with different email lengths to see what works best. Some audiences prefer short and sweet emails that get straight to the point, while others respond better to longer, more detailed emails that provide more information.

In addition to format and length, you can also test the content of your emails. This includes the messaging, tone, and call-to-action. For example, you might try different subject lines to see which ones generate the most opens, or different email copy to see which messages resonate most with your subscribers. Testing different calls-to-action can also be valuable, as it can help you determine what motivates your subscribers to take action. By testing these variables and analyzing the results, you can identify the most effective strategies for engaging your audience and driving conversions.

By creating engaging email content that provides value, uses visuals, is short and conversational, includes a clear call-to-action, and is tested and analysed, you can keep your subscribers interested and motivated to take action. Remember to always focus on meeting the needs and interests of your audience, and you'll be well on your way to creating effective email campaigns. Creating engaging email content is essential for the success of your email marketing campaigns.

Chapter 17: Segmenting Your Email List

As your email list grows, it's important to ensure that your campaigns are targeted and relevant to your subscribers. One way to achieve this is through segmentation. Segmenting your email list involves dividing your subscribers into smaller groups based on shared characteristics or behaviors. This allows you to send more personalized and targeted email campaigns, which can lead to increased engagement, higher open rates, and ultimately, more conversions.

Segmentation can be based on a variety of factors, including demographics, location, past purchase behavior, website activity, and email engagement. For example, you could segment your list based on age, gender, or location to send targeted promotions or content that is specific to each group. Or, you could segment based on past purchase behavior, sending customized emails that offer complementary products or services to previous purchases.

Segmentation can also help you to identify inactive subscribers or those who may be at risk of unsubscribing. By identifying these groups, you can send targeted re-engagement campaigns to encourage them to become active again or offer them an incentive to stay subscribed. With the right segmentation strategy, you can improve the performance of your email campaigns and achieve better results for your business.

Segmenting your email list can be done in several ways, depending on your business goals and the characteristics of your subscribers. Here are some common methods for segmenting your email list:

Demographics

Demographic segmentation is one of the most common and straightforward ways to segment your email list. This type of segmentation involves dividing your subscribers based on demographic information such as age, gender, location, and job title.

Knowing your subscribers' basic information can help you create more targeted and personalized email content that speaks directly to their needs and interests. For instance, if you are running an online clothing store, you might segment your email list based on gender or age. By doing so, you can send targeted emails featuring clothing items that are more likely to appeal to that particular group of customers.

Location-based segmentation can be particularly useful for businesses that have a physical store presence. You can send targeted emails to subscribers in specific geographical locations, promoting in-store events, local discounts, or even weather-specific products. Job title segmentation can also be useful for businesses that offer B2B services or products. You can send targeted emails to specific job titles or industries, showcasing how your offerings can help them solve their unique challenges.

Behaviour

Segmenting your email list based on behavior is a powerful way to improve your email marketing campaigns' effectiveness. By grouping subscribers according to their previous interactions with your brand, you can deliver targeted and personalized messaging that speaks directly to their interests and needs.

One effective way to segment by behavior is to track previous purchases. By analyzing purchase history, you can identify customers who have bought specific products or product categories and use this information to create tailored campaigns that promote similar products or complementary offerings. For example, if a customer has purchased a book on healthy eating, you could send them targeted emails promoting other health and wellness products or healthy recipe books.

Another way to segment based on behavior is by website activity. By tracking the pages a subscriber has visited on your website or how long they have spent on your site, you can infer their interests and create campaigns that are more likely to resonate with them. For example, if a subscriber has spent time on your website's fitness section, you could send them emails promoting fitness products or workout plans.

Email engagement is another important behavior to consider when segmenting your list. By analyzing which emails a subscriber has opened, clicked, or ignored, you can get a sense of their interests and preferences and create campaigns that cater to them. For example, if a subscriber has opened every email promoting sales but ignored emails promoting new product launches, you could send them more sales-related emails and fewer product launch announcements.

Overall, segmenting your email list based on behavior can help you deliver more personalized and targeted messaging to your subscribers, leading to increased engagement and conversions. By using the right tools and tracking subscriber behavior, you can effectively segment your list and create campaigns that are tailored to each group's interests and needs.

Interests

Segmenting your email list based on interests is a powerful way to personalize your email campaigns and make them more relevant to your subscribers. By tracking which topics your subscribers have shown interest in or engaged with in the past, you can create targeted campaigns that appeal directly to their preferences.

One way to gather data on your subscribers' interests is to track their behavior on your website or social media channels. For example, you can use tools like Google Analytics or Facebook Insights to see which pages or posts they have interacted with or which topics they have searched for.

Another way to gather data on your subscribers' interests is to simply ask them. You can use surveys or polls to gather feedback on what topics they are interested in, what types of content they prefer, and how frequently they want to receive emails from you. This information can help you create campaigns that are tailored to their specific interests and preferences.

Once you have identified the interests of your subscribers, you can create targeted campaigns that are designed to appeal directly to each group. For example, if you run a fashion blog and you have identified a group of subscribers who are interested in sustainable fashion, you can create campaigns that highlight eco-friendly clothing options or promote brands that are committed to sustainability. By tailoring your campaigns to the specific interests of each group, you can increase engagement and build stronger relationships with your subscribers.

Purchase history

Segmenting your email list based on purchase history can provide valuable insights into your customers' behavior and help you create personalized email campaigns that speak directly to their interests and needs. By analyzing past purchases, you can identify which products or services a particular subscriber is interested in and use that information to send more targeted and relevant email campaigns.

One effective way to use purchase history to segment your email list is by sending follow-up emails. These emails can be used to thank customers for their purchase, provide them with additional information about the product or service, or ask for feedback or a review. This not only helps to build a positive relationship with the customer but can also encourage repeat purchases.

Another way to leverage purchase history in email segmentation is by using it to send upsell or cross-sell offers. If a customer has recently purchased a product or service, you can use their purchase history to recommend complementary or related products that they might be interested in. This can help to increase the lifetime value of each customer and encourage them to make additional purchases.

Lastly, segmenting based on purchase history can also be useful for sending targeted promotions or discounts. For example, if you have a new product launch or a limited-time sale, you can send a promotion to subscribers who have previously purchased similar products. This helps to ensure that your email campaigns are relevant to each subscriber and can increase the chances of them making a purchase.

Overall, segmenting your email list based on purchase history can be a powerful tool for improving the effectiveness of your email campaigns. By using purchase history to create more personalized and relevant email content, you can increase engagement, improve customer relationships, and ultimately drive more conversions for your business.

Engagement

Segmenting based on engagement involves grouping subscribers based on their level of interaction with your emails. By targeting subscribers who are the most active and engaged, you can increase the chances of conversion and build stronger relationships with your audience.

One way to segment based on engagement is to group subscribers based on their email open rates. You can create a segment for subscribers who consistently open your emails and engage with your content. This segment can be used to send personalized content, exclusive promotions, and offers to reward their loyalty.

Another way to segment based on engagement is to group subscribers based on their click-through rates (CTR). By creating a segment for subscribers who have clicked on links within your emails, you can send them more targeted content and offers related to their interests. For example, if a subscriber clicks on a link to a specific product or service, you can send them follow-up emails with more information, offers, or promotions related to that product or service.

Additionally, segmenting based on engagement can also include identifying subscribers who have not opened or clicked on your emails in a while. These subscribers may need to be re-engaged with a targeted win-back campaign to encourage them to become active again. By sending targeted emails with exclusive promotions or personalized content, you can entice inactive subscribers to re-engage with your brand and increase the chances of a conversion.

Overall, segmenting based on engagement can help you target the subscribers who are most interested in your brand, increase engagement, and ultimately boost conversions. By understanding their interests and behaviours, you can provide them with more relevant and personalized content

Segmenting your email list is a crucial step in creating effective email campaigns. By dividing your subscribers into smaller groups based on shared characteristics, behaviours, and interests, you can personalize your email content and increase the relevance of your campaigns. This, in turn, can lead to higher engagement and conversions.

Remember, there are various ways to segment your email list, including demographics, purchase history, engagement, and interests. Use the segmentation criteria that best aligns with your business goals and target audience. Also, consider combining different segmentation criteria to create more specific segments.

Once you have segmented your email list, personalize your email content by using the subscriber's name, location, and other relevant information. This can help increase the subscriber's engagement and make them feel valued. Additionally, make sure to test and analyze your strategies regularly to determine what works best for your audience.

In conclusion, segmentation is an essential element of a successful email marketing strategy. By tailoring your email campaigns to specific segments of your audience, you can improve the relevance and effectiveness of your campaigns, leading to increased engagement, conversions, and ultimately, revenue. So, take the time to segment your email list and see the difference it can make in your email marketing campaigns.

Chapter 18: A/B Testing Your Emails

A/B testing is an effective way to determine what works best for your audience and improve the performance of your email campaigns. By creating two versions of an email campaign with one differing element and testing them against each other, you can gain insights into what resonates with your subscribers and make data-driven decisions to optimize your campaigns.

The differing element can be anything from the subject line, email copy, call-to-action, images, or even the sender's name. By testing different variables, you can identify which elements have the most significant impact on your subscribers' behaviour, such as open rates, click-through rates, and conversion rates.

One of the significant benefits of A/B testing is that it allows you to experiment with different ideas and strategies without risking your entire email list. Instead, you can test small changes and then use the results to optimize your email content and design further. This approach can help you increase engagement, conversions, and ultimately, revenue.

However, it's essential to keep in mind that A/B testing requires careful planning and execution. You need to ensure that you are testing only one variable at a time, or else you won't be able to determine which element is responsible for the changes in your campaign's performance. Additionally, you need to test each version on a similar sample size and for the same duration to eliminate any biases or variations.

In summary, A/B testing is a powerful tool that can help you improve the effectiveness of your email campaigns by allowing you to experiment with different ideas and strategies. By analyzing the results of your tests, you can identify what works best for your audience and make data-driven decisions to optimize your campaigns.

Here are 6 steps to follow when A/B testing your emails:

1. **Test One Element at a Time.** To accurately determine the impact of each change you make to your email, test one element at a time. For example, test two subject lines with the same email content, rather than two different subject lines and two different email designs.

2. **Determine Your Goal.** Before you begin testing, determine your goal. Do you want to increase open rates, click-through rates, or conversions? This will help you decide which element to test and which metric to track.

3. **Choose a Segment to Test.** Choose a segment of your email list to test. This could be a small percentage of your list or a specific segment based on demographics or behaviour. Testing different segments can help you understand how different groups respond to your email campaigns.

4. **Test for a Reasonable Period.** Test your emails for a reasonable period, such as 24-48 hours, to ensure you have enough data to make an informed decision. Test your emails at the same time and on the same day to minimize external factors that could impact results.

5. **Analyse Your Results.** Analyse the results of your A/B test to determine which version of the email performed better. Look at metrics such as open rates, click-through rates, and conversions to determine the impact of the change.

6. **Implement the Winning Version.** Once you've determined the winning version of your email, implement it in your next campaign. Use the insights you gained from your A/B test to improve future campaigns and continue to optimize your email marketing strategy.

A/B testing your emails is an essential practice for any email marketer who wants to improve the performance of their campaigns. By following the six steps outlined in this chapter, you can create more effective email campaigns that engage and convert your subscribers.

It's important to remember that A/B testing is an ongoing process. You should continue to test and refine your campaigns over time to ensure that you're always improving. By testing one element at a time, determining your goal, choosing a segment to test, testing for a reasonable period, analyzing your results, and implementing the winning version in your next campaign, you can improve your email marketing strategy and drive better results.

Remember to keep your subscribers in mind throughout the process. The goal of A/B testing is to create campaigns that resonate with your audience and drive engagement and conversions. By listening to your subscribers' feedback and adjusting your campaigns accordingly, you can create more targeted and effective email campaigns that deliver real value to your subscribers. So start A/B testing your emails today and see how it can help you take your email marketing to the next level.

Chapter 19: Analysing Your Funnel Metrics

Analyzing your funnel metrics is an essential step in improving the performance of your marketing funnel. The process of analyzing these metrics involves measuring the effectiveness of your marketing strategies and identifying areas for improvement. By tracking and analyzing key metrics, you can gain valuable insights into how your funnel is performing and make data-driven decisions to optimize it for better results and identify areas for improvement. However, with so many metrics available, it can be challenging to know which ones to focus on. So, which ones do you have to focus on?

When analyzing your funnel metrics, there are several key metrics that you should track. By monitoring these metrics, you can determine how well your funnel is performing at each stage and identify any bottlenecks or areas that require optimization.

1. *Conversion Rate* Your conversion rate is the percentage of visitors who take the desired action in your funnel, such as making a purchase or filling out a form. This is a key metric to track as it directly measures the effectiveness of your funnel in converting visitors into customers.

2. *Traffic Source* Knowing where your traffic is coming from can help you optimize your funnel for those sources. Track which sources are driving the most traffic

to your funnel, and focus on optimizing your funnel for those sources.

3. **Time on Site** Tracking the amount of time visitors spend on your site can give you insight into how engaged they are with your content. Longer time on site could indicate higher engagement and interest in your offer.

4. **Bounce Rate** Your bounce rate is the percentage of visitors who leave your site without taking any action. A high bounce rate could show a problem with your landing page or offer, and it may be necessary to make some adjustments to improve the user experience.

5. **Average Order Value** Tracking the average value of each purchase can help you determine if there are opportunities to increase sales by upselling or cross-selling additional products or services.

6. **Cost Per Acquisition (CPA)** Your cost per acquisition measures the amount of money spent on advertising and marketing efforts to acquire a new customer. Tracking your CPA can help you optimize your marketing spend and ensure that you are generating a positive return on investment.

Analyzing your funnel metrics is critical to understanding the effectiveness of your marketing strategies and identifying areas for improvement. However, tracking and analyzing metrics can be a daunting task, especially if you're not familiar with the tools available to help you do it. Fortunately, there are several tools available to make the process easier and more effective.

One of the most popular tools for tracking funnel metrics is Google Analytics. This free tool helps you track website traffic and user behavior, allowing you to gain insights into how visitors are interacting with your website. You can use Google Analytics to set up conversion goals and track your funnel metrics such as bounce rate, time on site, and conversion rate. Additionally, it allows you to create custom reports and dashboards to monitor your funnel performance over time.

For businesses that rely heavily on email marketing, tools like Mailchimp can help you track your funnel metrics for email campaigns. These tools allow you to track open rates, click-through rates, conversion rates, and other key metrics to help you understand how your email campaigns are performing. Additionally, they provide insights into subscriber behavior and engagement, allowing you to create targeted and personalized campaigns that resonate with your audience.

If you're running paid advertising campaigns, Google Ads and Facebook Ads Manager can help you track your funnel metrics for ad campaigns. These tools allow you to track impressions, clicks, conversions, and other key metrics to help you understand the performance of your ads. Additionally, they provide insights into audience demographics and behavior, allowing you to refine your targeting and optimize your ads for better results.

It's important to choose a tool that fits your specific needs and goals, and that integrates with the other tools you're using in your marketing stack. With the right tools in place, you can gain valuable insights into how your funnel is performing and make data-driven decisions to optimize it for better results.

In conclusion, tracking and analyzing your funnel metrics is critical to the success of your marketing strategies. By using the right tools, you can gain valuable insights into how your funnel is performing and make data-driven decisions to optimize it for better results. Use this data to make data-driven decisions to improve your conversion rates, increase your revenue, and grow your business.

Whether you're tracking website traffic, email campaigns, or paid advertising, there are tools available to help you track and analyze your funnel metrics effectively. So, take the time to find the tools that work best for you and start optimizing your funnel for better results.

Chapter 20: Using Retargeting Ads to Re-engage Leads

Retargeting ads are a popular form of online advertising that allows you to target users who have previously interacted with your website or content but have not yet converted. When someone visits your website, a small piece of code known as a pixel is placed on their browser. This pixel tracks their behavior on your site, such as the pages they visit, the actions they take, and the products or services they view. Based on this information, you can create targeted ads that will appear on other websites they visit, reminding them of your brand and offering.

Retargeting ads are highly effective because they target users who have already shown interest in your brand, products, or services. By reaching out to these warm leads, you have a higher chance of re-engaging them and converting them into customers. Retargeting ads can also help to increase brand awareness and recognition, as users are repeatedly exposed to your ads and become more familiar with your brand.

There are different types of retargeting ads that you can use to reach your target audience. One popular method is to create ads that feature the exact product or service that the user viewed on your website. This type of ad is highly personalized and reminds the user of the product or service they were interested in, encouraging them to return and complete the purchase.

Imagine you are running an online store that sells sporting equipment. A potential customer visits your website and browses through your selection of football balls, but leaves without making a purchase. You can then use retargeting ads to remind them of the football balls they were interested in and encourage them to return and complete the purchase.

You could create a retargeting ad that features a selection of football balls, including the exact ones that the user viewed on your website. The ad could include a message such as "Don't miss out on the perfect football ball for your game. Return to our store and complete your purchase today!" The ad could also offer a discount or free shipping to incentivize the user to return and make a purchase.

By using retargeting ads, you can stay top of mind with potential customers and encourage them to come back and complete their purchase. This can increase your conversion rates and ultimately drive more sales for your business.

Another type of retargeting ad is the dynamic retargeting ad, which features a carousel of products or services that the user previously viewed or expressed interest in. This type of ad is highly engaging and helps to showcase a variety of products or services that the user may be interested in, increasing the chances of conversion.

An example of this is when a user visits an e-commerce website and view several products, but does not complete a purchase. The website can use dynamic retargeting ads to show the user a carousel of the products they previously viewed. For example, if the user was interested in a pair of running shoes, a workout shirt, and a water bottle, the dynamic retargeting ad could show a carousel of those products, along with related items, such as other running shoes, workout clothes, and hydration products.

Each product in the carousel would be accompanied by an image, a brief description, and a price. The user could click on any product to view more details or add it to their cart. This type of ad is highly effective because it shows the user a range of products that are tailored to their interests and preferences. Additionally, it makes it easy for the user to complete the purchase by providing direct links to the product pages.

Overall, dynamic retargeting ads are a powerful way to engage with leads who have shown interest in your products or services, and to encourage them to complete a purchase. By featuring a carousel of personalized products or services, you can increase the chances of conversion and drive revenue for your business.

In addition to these types of retargeting ads, you can also use retargeting to upsell or cross-sell products to existing customers. By showing ads for complementary products or services, you can encourage repeat purchases and increase customer lifetime value.

For example, a customer who recently purchased a camera online may be retargeted with ads featuring camera accessories such as lenses, tripods, or camera bags. This can encourage the customer to make additional purchases and increase their overall value to the business.

To create effective retargeting ads, it's important to have a clear understanding of your target audience and their behavior on your website. You should also consider the timing and frequency of your ads to avoid overwhelming users with too many ads. By using retargeting ads strategically, you can increase conversions, drive revenue, and build stronger relationships with your customers. Additionally, make sure your ads are relevant to the user and provide value to them.

Retargeting ads are a proven way to boost your sales and engagement rates. By reminding potential customers of your products or services and displaying complementary offerings, you can increase your chances of conversion and maximize your revenue. Remember to test different ad formats and messaging, and to target the right audience at the right time. By integrating retargeting ads into your overall marketing strategy, you can create a cohesive funnel that guides leads from awareness to purchase. Keep in mind that retargeting ads work best as part of a larger, multi-channel approach, and that you should always measure and analyze your results to optimize your campaigns for even better results.

Chapter 21: Implementing Effective Follow-Up Sequences

Effective follow-up sequences are an essential component of any successful marketing strategy. They provide businesses with an opportunity to keep their leads engaged, build trust, and guide them towards a purchase decision. By delivering timely, relevant, and personalized messages to their leads, companies can establish a meaningful connection with them and establish a strong relationship that lasts beyond the initial contact. A well-designed follow-up sequence can help you move your leads through the sales funnel, overcome objections, and ultimately, increase your chances of converting them into loyal customers.

To put it simply, follow-up sequences are a series of automated messages that are sent to your leads over a period of time. These messages are designed to provide value, build trust, and move your leads closer to making a purchase. By implementing effective follow-up sequences, you can ensure that your leads receive consistent communication from your brand, even if they are not yet ready to buy.

Follow-up sequences can take many forms, from a series of emails to SMS messages or even direct mail. The key is to create a sequence that is tailored to your audience and their specific needs and interests. For example, if you're a B2B software company, your follow-up sequence might include a series of educational emails that provide valuable information about the benefits of your product and how it can help solve common pain points in the industry.

Effective follow-up sequences are not just about selling, but also about building a relationship with your leads. By providing value and showing genuine interest in their needs, you can establish yourself as a trusted authority in your industry and increase the likelihood of conversion when the time is right.

Implementing effective follow-up sequences involves several key steps, including:

Define Your Goals

Defining your goals is the first and most crucial step in implementing effective follow-up sequences. It's important to have a clear understanding of what you want to achieve with your follow-up sequences, as this will guide the content and structure of your sequences.

To get started, ask yourself what you want your follow-up sequences to accomplish. Is your goal to increase sales, build trust with your leads, educate them about your product or service, or something else entirely? Be specific and define your goals in measurable terms. For example, if your goal is to increase sales, consider how many sales you want to generate from your follow-up sequences and over what timeframe.

Once you have a clear understanding of your goals, you can start creating your follow-up sequences with those goals in mind. Your content and messaging should be designed to align with your goals and move your leads closer to taking the desired action.

For example, if your goal is to increase sales, your follow-up sequences should focus on educating your leads about your product or service, highlighting its benefits, and addressing any concerns they may have. You may also want to include promotional offers or discounts to encourage them to make a purchase.

On the other hand, if your goal is to build trust with your leads, your follow-up sequences should focus on providing value and establishing your expertise. This may involve sharing educational content, providing tips and advice, or offering free resources that your leads will find helpful.

Overall, defining your goals is a critical first step in implementing effective follow-up sequences. By aligning your content and messaging with your goals, you can create sequences that are tailored to your specific objectives and are more likely to achieve the desired results.

Figure out Your Frequency

Finding the right frequency for your follow-up sequences is crucial to keeping your leads engaged without overwhelming them. Too few follow-ups and your leads may forget about your offer, while too many can come across as pushy and lead to unsubscribes or lost sales.

To determine the best frequency for your follow-up sequences, consider your industry and the type of offer you're promoting. For example, a high-ticket item like a car or a house may require more time for decision-making, while a lower-priced product like a book or an online course may have a shorter decision-making cycle.

It's important to strike a balance between staying top of mind and respecting your leads' time and attention. A good rule of thumb is to follow up once a week or every two weeks, depending on the nature of your offer and your industry. However, it's also important to pay attention to your engagement metrics, such as open and click-through rates, and adjust your frequency accordingly. If you notice a drop in engagement, it may be time to reduce the frequency of your follow-ups or re-evaluate your content strategy.

In addition to the frequency of your follow-ups, it's also important to vary your messaging and content to keep your leads engaged. Avoid sending the same email over and over again, as this can lead to boredom and disengagement. Instead, offer a mix of valuable content, personalized offers, and social proof to keep your leads interested and motivated to take action.

Another important factor to consider when implementing effective follow-up sequences is segmenting your email list. By grouping your subscribers based on demographics, behavior, and interests, you can personalize your follow-up sequences and increase your chances of conversion. For example, you may want to send different follow-up sequences to new subscribers versus long-time subscribers, or to subscribers who have shown interest in a specific product or service.

Ultimately, the key to implementing effective follow-up sequences is to put yourself in your leads' shoes and consider their needs and preferences. By providing valuable content, respecting their time and attention, and personalizing your messaging, you can build trust and credibility with your leads and increase your chances of converting them into loyal customers.

Craft Your Content

To implement effective follow-up sequences, it's important to create content that resonates with your leads and provides value. Your content should be informative, engaging, and valuable to your leads. One of the key things to keep in mind is that you need to provide content that addresses their pain points and solves their problems.

Consider using a mix of content types, such as emails, videos, and social media posts, to keep your follow-up sequences fresh and interesting. For example, you might send a welcome email when someone signs up for your newsletter or subscribes to your service. In that email, you could provide an overview of what they can expect from your content, highlight some of your best content, and encourage them to follow you on social media.

Once someone has been on your list for a few weeks or months, it's time to start sending them more targeted content. For example, if you run a fitness website and someone has shown interest in weight loss, you might send them an email series on healthy eating habits or offer a discount on a fitness program that includes a personalized meal plan.

It's important to keep your content focused on the benefits of your offer and how it can solve your leads' pain points. Avoid being too salesy or pushy, and instead focus on building a relationship with your leads. This can be achieved by providing valuable content that educates and informs them about your product or service.

Another effective way to create follow-up sequences is to provide exclusive content to your subscribers. For instance, you could create a special webinar or video series that's only available to your subscribers. This will not only provide value to your subscribers, but also encourage them to stay engaged with your brand.

Finally, make sure to track and analyze the performance of your follow-up sequences regularly. This will help you identify what's working and what's not, and make data-driven decisions to optimize your campaigns for better results. By providing high-quality content, targeting your leads' pain points, and tracking your results, you can create effective follow-up sequences that nurture your leads over time and increase your chances of converting them into customers.

Personalize Your Messages

Personalization is a crucial element in implementing effective follow-up sequences. By using your leads' names and other relevant information, you can create a more personalized message that resonates with them on an individual level. Personalized messages feel more tailored to the recipient, which can help to establish trust and build rapport with your leads.

Segmenting your list based on interests or behaviors can also help you personalize your follow-up sequences. By grouping your leads into segments based on their interests or behaviors, you can tailor your messages to their specific needs and preferences. This level of personalization can lead to higher engagement and conversion rates, as your messages will be more relevant and useful to your leads.

To effectively segment your list, you can use various tools such as surveys or lead magnets to gather information about your leads. You can also analyze their behavior on your website, social media channels, and email interactions to better understand their interests and preferences.

Once you have segmented your list, you can create follow-up sequences that speak directly to each segment's interests and needs. For example, if you have a segment of leads interested in a particular product or service, you can create a follow-up sequence that provides more information about that product or service, addresses any common concerns or objections, and highlights its unique features and benefits.

In addition to personalization and segmentation, effective follow-up sequences should also have a clear and compelling call-to-action (CTA). Your CTA should be specific and relevant to the message and segment of the list you are targeting. For example, if you are sending a follow-up sequence to leads who have abandoned their cart, your CTA could be to complete the purchase or offer a discount code to incentivize them to come back and make the purchase.

Finally, it is important to track and analyze the performance of your follow-up sequences. By tracking key metrics such as open rates, click-through rates, and conversion rates, you can gain insights into what is working and what is not. You can then make data-driven decisions to optimize your follow-up sequences for better performance and higher conversions.

In conclusion, personalization, segmentation, clear and compelling CTAs, and tracking and analyzing performance are all critical components of effective follow-up sequences. By implementing these best practices, you can create follow-up sequences that engage, nurture, and convert your leads into customers.

Test and Refine

Once you have set up your follow-up sequences and personalized your messages, it's important to continually monitor and analyze their performance. This will help you identify any gaps or opportunities for improvement, and make data-driven decisions to optimize your sequences for better results.

One of the key metrics to track is the open rate, which indicates how many of your emails are being opened by your leads. A low open rate could indicate that your subject lines are not compelling enough or that your messages are ending up in spam folders. You can test different subject lines and adjust your messaging to improve your open rates.

Another important metric is the click-through rate, which measures how many people are clicking on the links in your emails. A low click-through rate could indicate that your messaging or calls-to-action are not resonating with your leads. You can test different messaging and CTAs to improve your click-through rates.

Finally, the conversion rate is a key metric to track in order to determine how many leads are actually converting into customers. A low conversion rate could indicate that your messaging or offer is not compelling enough, or that there are other barriers to conversion that need to be addressed. You can test different offers and messaging to improve your conversion rates.

By continually monitoring and analyzing these metrics, you can make data-driven decisions to optimize your follow-up sequences for better results. This may involve adjusting the frequency or timing of your messages, testing different messaging and offers, or segmenting your list further based on interests or behaviours.

It's also important to remember that effective follow-up sequences are not set in stone. Your business and your audience will evolve over time, and so should your follow-up sequences. Don't be afraid to experiment with new approaches or messaging and continue to test and refine your sequences for optimal results.

Effective follow-up sequences are crucial to any successful funnel and can significantly improve your conversion rates. By personalizing your messages, segmenting your list, and testing and refining your sequences over time, you can create a powerful system for nurturing your leads and building trust with your audience. Remember to track your metrics and adjust your content and frequency as needed to optimize your results. With a little planning and effort, your follow-up sequences can become a valuable asset in growing your business and reaching your marketing goals.

Chapter 22: Building Relationships with Your Customers

Building and nurturing strong relationships with your customers is critical to the long-term success of your business. A loyal customer base not only leads to repeat business but also can become a valuable source of referrals and positive reviews. The foundation of a strong customer relationship is trust, and trust is built over time through consistent communication, personalized interactions, and exceptional customer service. When your customers trust you, they are more likely to choose your brand over your competitors and recommend your products or services to others.

So, how do you go about building and nurturing these relationships? It starts with understanding your customers' needs and preferences. By gathering information about your customers, such as their demographics, interests, and purchasing history, you can tailor your communication and service to meet their specific needs. Personalization is a key element in building a strong customer relationship, and it can be achieved through various channels, such as email marketing, social media, and customer service interactions.

Another important aspect of building a strong customer relationship is consistency. Consistency in your communication, branding, and service builds trust and helps to establish your business as a reliable and dependable option for your customers. This consistency should be maintained across all touchpoints, from your website and social media to your email marketing and in-store experience.

Exceptional customer service is also a critical element in building strong customer relationships. A positive customer service experience can leave a lasting impression and build trust with your customers. Responding promptly to customer inquiries, providing helpful information, and going above and beyond to address customer needs can all contribute to a positive customer service experience.

In addition to personalized communication, consistency, and exceptional customer service, offering loyalty programs and other incentives can also help to build strong customer relationships. Loyalty programs, such as reward points or discounts for repeat purchases, can encourage customers to return and increase their loyalty to your brand.

Overall, building strong customer relationships requires a comprehensive and consistent approach. By understanding your customers' needs and preferences, personalizing your communication and service, maintaining consistency across all touchpoints, providing exceptional customer service, and offering incentives, you can create a loyal customer base that will support your business for years to come.

Chapter 23: Encouraging Referrals and Reviews

Encouraging referrals and reviews from your satisfied customers is a great way to amplify your marketing efforts and attract new business. As mentioned earlier, word-of-mouth marketing is one of the most effective forms of advertising, and referrals from existing customers can lead to high-quality leads and conversions. Here's how to encourage referrals and reviews:

Supply Excellent Customer Service

Providing excellent customer service is essential for building a strong relationship with your customers and establishing a successful referral or review program. When customers have a great experience with your business, they are more likely to recommend it to their friends, family, and colleagues. In contrast, if they encounter poor customer service, they may share negative feedback with others, which can harm your business's reputation.

To provide excellent customer service, it's essential to listen to your customers and address their concerns promptly. Make sure your customer service team is trained to handle any issues professionally and empathetically. Ensure that they have access to the information and resources necessary to resolve customer issues quickly and effectively.

Another way to provide excellent customer service is to offer proactive support. Reach out to your customers proactively to check in on their experience and see if they need any assistance. This can help you catch any issues early and resolve them before they escalate, showing your customers that you care about their experience and value their business.

Providing excellent customer service is a foundation for encouraging referrals and reviews. When customers feel valued and cared for, they are more likely to share their positive experiences with others. By focusing on delivering exceptional service and addressing any concerns quickly and professionally, you can build a loyal customer base that will be happy to refer your business to others and leave positive reviews.

Ask for Referrals and Reviews

Asking for referrals and reviews is a common and effective practice in the world of marketing. It is important to remember that satisfied customers are often more than willing to provide referrals and leave positive reviews if they are asked to do so. Including a call-to-action in your email campaigns or on your website can be a great way to encourage customers to share their positive experiences with others. Make sure to keep the request simple and specific, and provide clear instructions on where and how to leave a review.

You can also offer incentives to customers who refer new business to your company or leave a review. This can be in the form of a discount, a free trial, or other perks that your customers will find valuable. However, be careful not to incentivize customers to leave only positive reviews, as this can come across as inauthentic and may harm your credibility.

In addition to asking for referrals and reviews, you can also make it easy for customers to refer others or leave a review. Include links to your social media pages and review sites on your website and in your email campaigns. You can also create a dedicated landing page for referrals and reviews, providing all the necessary information and links in one place.

Overall, encouraging referrals and reviews is a powerful way to grow your business and build strong relationships with your customers. By providing exceptional customer service and making it easy for customers to refer others and leave reviews, you can create a loyal customer base that will help your business thrive.

Incentivize Referrals

Offering incentives to customers who refer their friends or family to your business can be an effective way to encourage more referrals. These incentives can be in the form of discounts, gift cards, or other rewards. For example, you could offer a referral discount code that the customer can share with their friends, which would give both the referrer and the new customer a discount on their purchase.

Another approach is to offer a reward to customers who refer a certain number of new customers to your business. For example, you could offer a gift card or free product for every five referrals that a customer sends your way. This not only incentivizes your customers to refer more people but also rewards them for their loyalty and support.

It's important to make sure that any incentives you offer are reasonable and aligned with your business goals. You don't want to offer discounts or rewards that are too generous and end up hurting your bottom line. However, when done correctly, offering incentives for referrals can be a win-win situation for both you and your customers.

Make it Easy to Leave a Review

Making it easy for your customers to leave a review is crucial in encouraging them to do so. Including links to your review pages on your website, social media accounts, and email signature can greatly increase the likelihood of customers leaving a review. Additionally, it is important to make the review process as simple and straightforward as possible. Consider providing clear instructions on how to leave a review and what customers can expect from the process.

Another way to make leaving a review easy is to offer multiple review platforms for customers to choose from. Not everyone uses the same review sites, so providing options like Google, Yelp, or Facebook can accommodate a wider range of customers.

It's also important to follow up with customers after they have left a review, whether positive or negative. Thank them for their feedback and address any issues or concerns they may have mentioned. This demonstrates that you value their opinion and are committed to providing excellent customer service.

Overall, making the review process as easy as possible and following up with customers can help encourage them to leave a review and contribute to the growth of your business.

Respond to Reviews

Responding to reviews is an essential aspect of managing your online reputation and building trust with your customers. When you respond to both positive and negative reviews, you show your customers that you value their feedback and are committed to providing excellent service.

When responding to positive reviews, take the time to thank the customer for their kind words and express your appreciation for their business. This will not only make the customer feel valued but will also encourage them to continue supporting your business.

On the other hand, responding to negative reviews requires a different approach. First and foremost, it's essential to stay professional and avoid becoming defensive. Start by thanking the customer for their feedback and acknowledging their concerns. Then, offer a solution or explanation to address their issue. By doing so, you show that you take their feedback seriously and are committed to resolving any problems.

It's important to note that negative reviews are not necessarily a bad thing. They provide an opportunity to learn and improve your business. Responding to negative reviews in a constructive way can even turn a dissatisfied customer into a loyal one.

In summary, responding to reviews, both positive and negative, is an essential aspect of building trust with your customers and managing your online reputation. It shows that you value their feedback and are committed to providing excellent service.

Referrals and reviews have become an essential part of any marketing strategy. They not only help businesses build a strong reputation, but also attract new customers and increase brand awareness. With the rise of social media and online reviews, consumers are more likely to trust the opinions of their peers than traditional advertising. Therefore, having a solid referral and review program is crucial for any business looking to succeed in today's competitive market.

One effective way to encourage referrals and reviews is to provide exceptional customer service. Satisfied customers are more likely to recommend your business to others and leave positive reviews. Therefore, investing in your customer service team and training them to provide outstanding service can be an excellent way to boost your referral and review program. By consistently exceeding your customers' expectations, you'll not only create loyal customers but also encourage them to refer your business to their friends and family.

Another way to incentivize referrals and reviews is to offer exclusive rewards or discounts. This can be an effective way to motivate your customers to leave a review or refer their friends to your business. It also shows your customers that you value their feedback and appreciate their loyalty. Providing a simple and straightforward process for leaving a review, along with an incentive, can significantly increase the number of reviews you receive and help you stand out from the competition.

Finally, monitoring and responding to reviews is an essential aspect of any referral and review program. Not only does responding to reviews show your customers that you care about their feedback, but it also provides you with valuable insights into your business's strengths and weaknesses. Positive reviews can be used to promote your business, while negative reviews can be addressed and used as an opportunity to improve. By actively engaging with your customers' feedback, you can build a strong reputation, improve your customer experience, and attract new customers.

In conclusion, building a robust referral and review program is essential for any business looking to succeed in today's market. By providing excellent customer service, incentivizing referrals and reviews, making it easy to leave a review, and monitoring and responding to reviews, you can create a loyal customer base and attract new customers to your business. Referrals and reviews are a powerful tool that can help you stand out from the competition, and by prioritizing them in your marketing strategy, you can take your business to the next level.

Chapter 24: Scaling Your Funnel Marketing Efforts

Once you have a successful funnel in place, the next step is to scale your efforts to reach even more potential customers. Here are some tips for scaling your funnel marketing efforts:

Increase Your Ad Spend

When it comes to scaling your funnel marketing efforts, increasing your ad spend is one of the simplest and most straightforward ways to achieve that goal. By investing more money in your existing campaigns, you can reach a larger audience, generate more leads, and ultimately increase your sales and revenue. However, it's crucial to approach ad spend increases strategically to ensure that you're seeing a positive return on investment.

Before you increase your ad spend, it's essential to evaluate your existing campaigns' performance. Look at your metrics, such as click-through rates, conversion rates, and cost per acquisition, to determine which campaigns are delivering the best results. Focus on those campaigns that are already generating positive ROI, and consider scaling those first. By investing more money into campaigns that are already successful, you're more likely to see a positive return on investment from your increased ad spend.

When increasing your ad spend, it's also crucial to adjust your targeting strategy. As you reach a larger audience, you may find that your targeting needs to be refined to continue generating positive results. Consider segmenting your audience further to ensure that your ads are reaching the most relevant potential customers. For example, if you're advertising a high-end product, you may want to target customers who have a history of making luxury purchases.

Another essential consideration when scaling your ad spend is the competition. As you increase your ad spend, you may find that you're competing with other advertisers for the same audience. This can lead to increased competition and higher costs per click. To combat this, it's essential to continually monitor your metrics and adjust your strategy as needed. Consider testing different ad formats or targeting strategies to ensure that you're getting the most out of your increased ad spend.

Expand Your Audience

Expanding your reach to new audiences is a critical step in scaling your funnel marketing efforts. With so many different platforms and channels available, it can be overwhelming to decide where to focus your efforts. However, by understanding your target audience and exploring new platforms, you can increase your chances of reaching new potential customers.

One approach to expanding your reach is to explore new advertising channels. For example, if you're currently running Facebook ads, consider testing out other social media platforms like Instagram, Twitter, or LinkedIn. Each platform has a unique user base, and it's essential to understand how your target audience engages with each one. Instagram, for example, is popular among younger demographics, while LinkedIn is ideal for B2B marketing.

Another approach is to explore new content formats. For example, if you're primarily using blog posts and email marketing to reach your audience, consider experimenting with video or podcast content. Video content has exploded in popularity in recent years, and it's an effective way to engage with your audience visually. Podcasts are also an excellent way to build a loyal following and establish yourself as an authority in your industry.

In addition to exploring new channels and content formats, it's also essential to understand your target audience and their behavior. By analyzing data from your existing campaigns, you can gain insights into what's working and what's not. Use this information to inform your strategy for reaching new audiences.

One effective approach to understanding your target audience is to create buyer personas. A buyer persona is a fictional representation of your ideal customer based on market research and data. By understanding your buyer persona's interests, pain points, and behavior, you can create content and messaging that resonates with them.

Once you have a clear understanding of your target audience and their behavior, it's essential to create content that speaks directly to them. Personalization is key to building a strong relationship with your audience and increasing the chances of converting them into customers. Consider segmenting your list based on interests or behaviors and tailoring your messaging to each group.

Develop New Products or Services

One of the most effective ways to grow your business and scale your funnel is to develop new products or services that complement your existing offerings. Not only can this help you reach new customers, but it can also lead to increased sales from your existing customer base.

The key to developing complementary products or services is to understand your customers' needs and preferences. What problems are they facing that your current offerings don't address? What additional value could you provide that would make their lives easier or more enjoyable?

Once you have a clear understanding of your customers' needs, you can begin brainstorming new products or services that complement your existing offerings. This could involve expanding your product line to include related items or developing services that provide additional support or customization.

For example, if you own a company that sells fitness equipment, you might consider developing a line of workout supplements or offering personalized training plans. These offerings would not only appeal to your existing customer base but could also attract new customers who are looking for a more comprehensive approach to their fitness routine.

When developing complementary products or services, it's important to ensure that they align with your brand and values. You want to avoid diluting your brand or confusing your customers with unrelated offerings. Instead, focus on creating offerings that are in line with your current offerings and enhance your customers' experience with your brand.

Another key consideration when developing complementary products or services is pricing. You want to ensure that your pricing strategy is consistent with your current offerings and provides value to your customers. You may need to adjust your pricing strategy based on factors such as production costs, market demand, and competition.

Partner with Other Businesses

Collaboration is a powerful tool in any marketing strategy, and it can be especially beneficial in funnel marketing. When you partner with other businesses or influencers, you can leverage their expertise and audiences to expand your reach and attract new potential customers.

One of the most straightforward ways to collaborate with other businesses is to participate in cross-promotions. This involves partnering with a complementary business and promoting each other's products or services to your respective audiences. For example, a fitness studio might collaborate with a nutritionist to offer a joint promotion that encourages customers to sign up for both services. Cross-promotions can be a great way to expand your reach and attract new customers who are interested in related products or services.

Another way to collaborate with other businesses is to co-create content. This involves partnering with another business to create a piece of content that is relevant to both of your audiences. For example, a software company might collaborate with a marketing agency to create an ebook on how to build a successful marketing funnel. By working together, both businesses can reach a broader audience and establish themselves as thought leaders in their respective industries.

Influencer marketing is another powerful collaboration strategy that can help you reach new potential customers. By partnering with influencers who have a large and engaged following, you can tap into their audience and gain exposure to potential customers who may not have heard of your business before. When selecting influencers to work with, it's essential to choose individuals who are relevant to your industry and have a genuine connection with their audience. By working with influencers who share your values and are passionate about your products or services, you can build trust and credibility with their followers.

Another way to collaborate with influencers is to offer them exclusive access to your products or services in exchange for their promotion. This can be a great way to build buzz and excitement around your offerings and attract new potential customers who are interested in the influencer's recommendations.

When collaborating with other businesses or influencers, it's essential to establish clear goals and expectations upfront. Be sure to communicate your objectives, timelines, and any other relevant details to ensure that everyone is on the same page. You should also establish clear metrics for measuring success and track your results to determine the effectiveness of your collaborations.

In summary, collaborating with other businesses and influencers is a powerful way to expand your reach and attract new potential customers. By working together, you can tap into new audiences, share resources and expertise, and establish yourself as a thought leader in your industry. Whether you choose to participate in cross-promotions, co-create content, or leverage influencer marketing, the key is to establish clear goals and expectations upfront and track your results to determine the effectiveness of your collaborations.

Hire Additional Staff

As your business grows, so too will your funnel marketing efforts. As you attract more leads and convert more customers, you'll need to ensure that you have the resources in place to keep up with demand. This may mean hiring additional staff to help manage your funnel marketing efforts.

When considering adding staff to your team, it's important to assess where you need the most support. Do you need more marketers to help create and execute campaigns? Or do you need more salespeople to handle incoming leads and convert them into customers? Perhaps you need additional customer support staff to ensure that your customers are satisfied and happy with their experience.

Once you've identified your staffing needs, it's important to hire the right people. Look for individuals with relevant experience and a track record of success in their respective fields. Consider conducting thorough interviews and even providing skills tests to ensure that candidates have the necessary skills and knowledge to excel in their roles.

In addition to hiring additional staff, you may also want to consider outsourcing certain aspects of your funnel marketing efforts. For example, you may want to hire a freelance copywriter to create compelling email campaigns or a graphic designer to create eye-catching social media ads. Outsourcing can be a cost-effective way to access specialized talent and expertise without committing to full-time staff.

Of course, adding staff to your team comes with costs, including salaries, benefits, and training expenses. Before making any hires, it's important to carefully consider your budget and ensure that you have the financial resources to support additional staff. This may require adjusting your marketing budget or exploring alternative funding options, such as loans or grants.

Once you have the right staff in place, it's important to ensure that they have the necessary resources to succeed. This may include providing ongoing training and support, as well as access to the latest tools and technology. By investing in your staff, you can ensure that they are equipped to effectively manage and optimize your funnel marketing efforts.

Continuously Test and Optimize

In today's fast-paced digital landscape, staying up-to-date with the latest trends and technologies is crucial for any business looking to succeed with funnel marketing. Continuously testing and experimenting with new tactics can help you stay ahead of the curve and find new opportunities to attract and convert potential customers.

One of the most effective ways to stay ahead of the curve is to keep a close eye on industry trends and emerging technologies. For example, the rise of voice search and artificial intelligence is changing the way that consumers interact with brands online. By staying up-to-date with these trends and leveraging new technologies in your funnel marketing efforts, you can position yourself as a thought leader and stay ahead of the competition.

Another effective strategy for scaling your funnel is to continuously test and experiment with new tactics. For example, you could try out different ad formats, landing page designs, or lead magnets to see which ones are most effective at converting potential customers. By tracking key metrics such as click-through rates, conversion rates, and cost per acquisition, you can quickly identify which tactics are working and which ones need to be refined or replaced.

Another key aspect of scaling your funnel is to focus on building and nurturing strong relationships with your customers. This means providing exceptional customer service, personalized communication, and value-added content that resonates with your target audience. By creating a positive customer experience at every touchpoint, you can build trust and loyalty with your audience, leading to repeat business and referrals.

As the digital landscape continues to evolve, so too will funnel marketing. New technologies, platforms, and strategies will emerge, and businesses must be ready to adapt and experiment to stay ahead of the curve. However, some things will remain constant. Customer-focused marketing will always be essential, and providing value and building relationships will always be crucial to success.

Therefore, it's important to stay up-to-date with the latest trends and continuously experiment and optimize your campaigns. Regularly review your data to identify areas for improvement and adjust your strategies accordingly. For example, if you're not seeing the desired results from a particular stage of your funnel, consider testing different messaging or offers to see if you can improve your conversion rates.

In conclusion, scaling your funnel marketing efforts can help you reach a larger audience, generate more leads and sales, and grow your business. Increasing your ad spend, expanding your reach to new audiences, and leveraging partnerships are just a few ways to scale your efforts. By staying up-to-date with the latest trends and continuously testing and optimizing your campaigns, you can continue to attract and convert potential customers and achieve even greater success. Remember that funnel marketing is a journey, not a destination, and by staying committed to your goals and adapting to change, you can achieve long-term success.

Chapter 25: Conclusion and Future of Funnel Marketing

Funnel marketing is not just a trend, but a powerful way to attract, engage, and convert potential customers. By guiding them through a series of steps, businesses can build trust and supply value, ultimately leading to increased sales and revenue. However, as the digital landscape continues to evolve, funnel marketing will evolve with it. New technologies, platforms, and strategies will emerge, and businesses must be ready to adapt and experiment to stay ahead of the curve.

So, whether you're just starting with funnel marketing or are already an expert, the future is bright. By staying up-to-date with the latest trends and continuously experimenting and optimizing your campaigns, businesses can continue to attract and convert potential customers and grow their business.

Thank you for reading *The Ultimate Funnel Marketing Guide: Attract, Engage, and Convert Customers*. We hope that it has provided you with valuable insights and tools to take your funnel marketing to the next level. Remember, success in funnel marketing requires dedication, creativity, and a willingness to learn and adapt. Best of luck on your funnel marketing journey!